Wilt Thou Be Made Whole

For: Charlene, Willie Mae
Beloved of the Lord

Now there is at Jerusalem
by the sheep market
a pool, which is called
in the Hebrew tongue Bethesda,
having five porches.
In these lay a great multitude
of impotent folk,
of blind, halt, withered,
waiting for the moving of the water.
For an angel went down
at a certain season
into the pool,
and troubled the water:
whosoever then first
after the troubling of the water
stepped in
was made whole
of whatsoever disease he had.
And a certain man was there,
which had an infirmity
thirty and eight years.
When Jesus saw him lie,
and knew that he had been now
a long time in that case,
He saith unto him,
Wilt thou be made whole?
The impotent man answered Him,
Sir, I have no man,
when the water is troubled,
to put me into the pool:
but while I am coming,
another steppeth down before me.
Jesus saith unto him,
Rise, take up thy bed, and walk.
And immediately
the man was made whole,
and took up his bed,
and walked:
and on the same day
was the sabbath.

John 5:2-9

Wilt Thou Be Made Whole

ray bates

Star Books Inc.

lifting up the Light of the world

Wilson NC 27893

Library of Congress Cataloging-in-Publication Data:
Bates, Ray.
    Wilt thou be made whole? / Ray Bates.
        p.   cm.
    ISBN 0-915541-08-4 : $9.00
    1. Spiritual healing--Biblical teaching. 2. Jesus Christ--Person
and offices. 3. Bible. N.T. Gospels--Criticism, interpretation, etc.
I. Title.
BS2545.H4B37 1991
234' . 13--dc20   91-32633
                                                                    CIP

Cover art and design by Raymond W. Bates

Published by Star Books, inc.
408 Pearson Street
Wilson, NC 27893

Telephone: (919) 237-1591

ISBN: 0-915541-08-4

First printing

Contents

Contents

Introduction

Many of you will be made every whit whole as you read this book, not because anything of a miraculous nature is contained in its pages, but because your heart and your head will come to one unshakable conclusion: the revealed will of God is that *all* be healed, live in divine health and be whole of whatever ails them, no matter how dreaded or fearsome.

A good first step toward healing and divine health is to answer the question in the title of this book: *Wilt thou be made whole?* Does your heart's desire match His heart's desire for you? Is it your purpose to be healthy and whole? Is it your will? Here, a simple yes *out loud* will set the divine flow in motion; the Lord will surely honor it. His Word tells us He wishes to give us *the desires of our hearts* (Psalm 37:4), that if we will not doubt in our hearts, *we can have what we say* (Mark 11:23,24) and that if we will trust in Him and lean not to our own understanding, He will direct our paths toward divine health or whatever else we need (Proverbs 3:5-8).

Regardless of how you feel and where you stand with pills, doctors and hospitals, know this: thinking based on sense knowledge is wholly undependable. But when your focus is on the revealed will of God and His heart's desire that you be healed, made whole and live in unparalleled victory, your trust in Him is valuable and precious in His sight. He cannot but honor that trust.

The Victorious Life

In order for us to win the many battles and the war, we must know who our enemies are, the extent of their weaponry, their probable strategy and what is required to defeat them. It is also mandatory that we know and understand our weapons, their capabilities and deficiencies (if any), where our strength lies and the causes of any weaknesses that might exist. Finally, we must possess the wisdom of God (James 1:5) so that we can deploy our forces whenever and wherever needed in the swiftest, most dynamic and positive way. A well-planned surprise attack on even the most formidable enemy will often prove to be devastating and demoralizing for him.

The Word says "the weapons of our warfare are not carnal [fleshly or mechanical], but mighty through God to the pulling down of strongholds; casting down imaginations, and every high thing that exalteth itself against the knowledge of God, and bringing into captivity every thought to the obedience of Christ" (2 Corinthians 10:4,5). Also, "The Word of God is quick [life-giving], and powerful, and sharper than any two-edged sword, piercing even to the dividing asunder of soul and spirit, and of the joints and marrow, and is a discerner of the thoughts and intents of the heart" (Hebrews 4:12).

In Ephesians, Paul writes, "Be strong in the Lord, and in the power of His might. Put on the whole armor of God, that ye may be able to stand against the wiles [deceitfulness] of the devil" (Ephesians 6:10,11). Our enemy is the devil, much as Hitler was our enemy in World War II. If there had been no Hitler, would there have been a war? There is no way for us to speculate, of course, because we know Hitler existed. We must be equally aware of the existence of Satan. For although Hitler was the enemy we could focus on, we were literally at war with Germany and her allies, and our battles were fought with armies, corps, divisions, regiments, battalions, companies and squads--down to the individual enemy soldiers.

In the spirit world, the nation is spiritual Persia (Daniel 10) and Satan is its ruling prince, as was Hitler in Germany.

Now back to Ephesians, where it tells us the armies, corps and divisions we must fight: "For we wrestle not against flesh and blood, but against principalities, against powers, against the rulers of darkness of this world, against spiritual wickedness in high places [heavenlies]" (Ephesians 6:12). These are the forces commanded by spiritual Field Marshals, Generals and sub-Princes, while the individual enemies are demons and fallen angels that were thrown out of heaven with Satan.

This tells us why we must take unto ourselves the whole armor of God, that we may be able to withstand in the evil day, and having done all, to stand (see Ephesians 6:13). We are to stand staunch, defiant, immovable. Isn't that great and heartening? For if God commands us to do something, it is because He knows it is possible for us to do it. Though He is capable of recommending the unlikely, He never demands the impossible because He knows that nothing is impossible for Him.

Do you know that in the face of evil it is wisdom to stand? The reason is that when you know the strategies and weaknesses of your enemy, that your weapons are quicker, sharper and mightier, and that your armor is virtually impenetrable, there is no reason to even entertain the idea of surrender. Paul says, "Stand therefore, having your loins girt about with truth [that God is trustworthy], and having on the breastplate of righteousness [for God is holy]; and your feet shod with the preparation of the gospel of peace [being always ready with the Word to establish His kingdom]; above all, taking the shield of faith, wherewith ye shall be able to quench all the fiery darts of the wicked [standing before the *full force* of the enemy with the *full assurance* that nothing can by any means hurt you]. And take the helmet of salvation [which gives health, wholeness, deliverance and preservation] and the sword of the Spirit, which is the Word of God [by

which we speak those things which be not as though they are]: praying always with all prayer and supplication in the Spirit [thus keeping
in constant touch with our Supreme Commander, who knows every
move of the enemy]" (Ephesians 6:14-18a). Beloved, *that* is how we
can stand triumphant.

The Many Ways God Heals

In our experience and research, we have found twelve basic ways
God uses to heal His people:

1) by grace
2) by the laying on of hands
3) by faith
4) by deliverance
5) by obedience (or action)
6) by His Word
7) by compassion (or love)
8) by agreement
9) by believing (and receiving)
10) by prayer
11) by the Name of Jesus
12) by the sovereign working of the Holy Spirit (acting alone)

The reader is cautioned not to grab hold of any one of these as an
imperative, because a careful study will reveal there are ways within
ways that will allow you a whole loaf instead of a slice. Also, these
ways within ways will keep us from trying to box God in, insisting
that He do it our way.

As you move along through this book, a striking fact will
emerge: you will see that in all the ways Jesus used to heal, He made
provision for us to do likewise. Isn't that just too marvelous for
words? No matter what your individual need, Jesus has provided the
answer; no matter how complex the problem, He has given you the
solution; and no matter how painful or frightening your affliction,

He has provided (past tense) for your complete and perfect soundness. For His Word says "I *am* the Lord that healeth thee" (Exodus 15:26).

And now, let's begin.

1

Healing, Health and Wholeness
By the Grace, Goodness and Mercy of God

Grace and truth came
Read John 1:17

Grace and truth came, and the Bible tells us it came by Jesus Christ.
Isn't that a remarkable statement? Was not grace and truth in the
world before the coming of the Lord? Of course it was. Noah, Abraham, Isaac, Jacob, Joseph, Moses--nearly all the patriarchs and pro-
phets--found *grace* in the sight of the Lord God (Genesis 6:8). And
as to *truth,* the same patriarchs and prophets--e.g., Moses, David,
Solomon and Isaiah--were intimately acquainted with the truth of
God (see, e.g., Moses' "Hymn of Joy" in Deuteronomy 32, especially
verse 4).

How, then, can John say, "Grace and truth came by Jesus
Christ"?

For you who don't already know, *grace* is often defined as "unmerited [or unearned] favor." In light of man's values and limitations, that is not a bad definition. But when we consider the grace of
God and attempt to confine it in the framework of this definition,
the definition pales to the point of nearly fading completely away.
For the grace of God is quite literally His gift of love to us, which we
already know is boundless, as well as limitless. Describing God's
grace as "unmerited favor" is like defining *beautiful* as "looking fair to
middlin'." The definition really isn't good enough.

While we read that *faith* worketh by *love* (Galatians 5:6),
nowhere does the Bible say we must do anything to receive *grace*.

Grace is not an act of anything; it is the consummate result of love--
which, of course, is Jesus Christ, the Word of God, made flesh to
dwell among us (John 1:14). Although grace--and therefore, Jesus--
was freely given, like any of God's gifts it must be received, ap-
propriated or *taken unto ourselves* by an act of our wills. Otherwise it
is as useless as geometry to a toddler.

Thy sins be forgiven thee
Read Matthew 9:2-7; Mark 2:1-12; Luke 5:18-26

By its very Authorship, we can see that God's grace is exuberantly
unconfined and, like healing, is everywhere in all the earth. Only the
will of man can make its power of none effect. Only by his hardness
of heart and ignorance of God's plan for his life can man negate the
all-encompassing love that is the force behind His grace. Nothing, of
course, can stop God's love, because the Bible assures us He *is* love
(1 John 4:16). But if man continues to hold up his umbrella of sin to
ward off God's grace, which rains on the just and the unjust (Matthew 5:45), God's grace does not any less abound. It is just more difficult for the umbrella man to enter into its fullness of joy.

Again and again as God poured His marvelous grace through
Jesus Christ, multitudes were set free from oppression, sickness and
afflictions of every type and description. Numerous scriptures indi-
cate that *all* were healed (Matthew 4:23,24; 14:14,35,36; 15:30,31;
Mark 1:30-34; 3:1-5,10-14; 6:4-6; 9:17-29; 10:46-52; Luke 6:17-21;
John 4:46-54).

That very same grace Jesus exhibited in the above scriptures is
resident in every born-again Spirit-filled believer. For John said, "Of
His fulness have all we received, *and grace for grace.* For the law was
given by Moses, but grace and truth came by Jesus Christ" (John
1:16,17).

Since we know it is His desire that we give full expression to
His image in us, it is vital that we understand we are not waiting to
receive that grace but that it is already ours in the fullest measure
with a continuing flow as "grace for grace" suggests. Having thus

received, it is incumbent upon us to earnestly seek His guidance and
leading in the matter of how that grace can best be used and how
that use will be most pleasing to Him.

Probably one of the greatest acts of grace recorded in the Bible
concerns the man sick of the palsy who was let down through the
roof. For the Word says he was carried by four men who, seeing
there was no other way to get the sick man to Jesus, broke through
the roof and let him down in the midst. The Bible then says, "When
Jesus saw their faith, He said to the sick of the palsy, Son, thy sins be
forgiven thee."

Now, whether Jesus saw the faith of the four men who carried
the sick of the palsy or of the four carriers *and* the sick man is not of
any consequence here. Here we are dealing with *grace*. In a later
chapter, we will be dealing with the part *faith* played.

Unlike those who have not yet come into the fulness of discernment, Jesus didn't have to wonder whether sin was the problem: He
knew it. As a result, He didn't have to dance around with the symp-
tom--the paralysis; He could go right to the root cause--sin. How did
He do that? He simply forgave the man's sin, thereby releasing him
from the penalty and the bondage.

Of course this caused an emotional furor among the scribes
and Pharisees there in the room. They were outraged. For they said
within themselves, "Why doth this man thus speak blasphemies?
Who can forgive sins but God only?" Then the Bible declares, "Jesus
knowing their thoughts said, Wherefore *think ye evil in your hearts*?
For whether is easier, to say, Thy sins be forgiven thee; or to say,
Arise, and walk? But that ye may know that the *Son of man* hath
power on earth to forgive sins, (then saith He to the sick of the
palsy,) "Arise, take up thy bed, and go unto thine house" (Matthew
9:6).

That was Jesus illustrating *our authority* with regard to the forgiveness of sins. Here we are not dealing with *forgiveness* but with
grace. *Forgiveness* will be dealt with in detail in a later chapter. But
this is not to skirt the issue. We not only have the Lord's *permission*

to forgive sins, we have an out-and-out *commission*. For after commanding His disciples, "Receive ye the Holy Ghost," Jesus gives us His unalterable seal of approval: "Whose soever sins ye [meaning us] remit, they are remitted unto them" (John 20:23a).

Oh, what a word this is for the man or woman who needs to know. In the Greek, the words *remit* and *remission* are *aphiemi* and *aphesis*, which mean "deliverance, forgiveness, liberty, to forsake, lay aside, leave, let alone, let be, let go, put away, send away, suffer to be so." But the primary meanings come down to "forgive" or "forgiveness." So not only are we able to forgive the sins of others *in the Name of Jesus*, we are able to forgive ourselves, since we are just as much "whosoevers" as anyone else on earth.

Therefore, beloved, if you are suffering the consequences of sins, either yours or those of another, have you ever *repented* and asked the Lord's forgiveness? Or in taking an action according to His Word, have you ever gone before Him in humble supplication, asking the Father to guide and lead you by His Spirit into the perfect prayer?

Such a prayer might go something like this:

Father, in humble obedience to Your Word and in the Name of Jesus, I come before You for the purpose of remitting the sins of the entire world (which includes me). Since there is not one soul on earth who is not a whosoever, I accept the commission of the Lord Jesus to loose all men from the penalty and bondage of their sins, that they may, with complete liberty, hear and understand the Gospel of the kingdom. Father, that they may come before You this day, as I have, in the beauty of holiness, knowing it is by Your grace that I have been made the righteousness of God in Christ, whose holy Name I bless.   Amen--and Amen

Take My yoke upon you
Read Matthew 11:25-30

"Take My yoke upon you, and learn of Me; for I am meek and lowly in heart: and ye shall find rest unto your souls. For My yoke is easy, and My burden is light."

Jesus made this statement after prophesying the ultimate destruction of Chorazin, Bethsaida and Capernaum for their un-belief--also after thanking the Father that He had hidden these things from the wise and prudent, and revealed them unto babes.

Why would anyone wish to be yoked together with someone who is weak, mild and humble (which "meek and lowly of heart" im-plies)? How would you expect to fare? And if your own burden is al-ready too heavy, why would you even vaguely consider being joined with someone who has already confessed he is weaker than you?

Things like that are what make the Bible so outrageous; it ab-solutely defies human logic. A careful study of this scripture will reveal that Christ is not really taking your burden at all but is adding His to yours. Here I am, trying to unload my burden somewhere and the Lord exhorts me to take on His (even though light), so I can have rest for my soul! How can one reconcile taking on an additional burden so he can find rest? One can't, of course, for burdens are bur-dens and rest is rest.

Nevertheless, the Lord says, "Come unto Me, all ye that labour and are heavy laden, and I will give you rest." Outrageous? In my humanity I concede the point.

But it is our humanness that causes us to err. We tend to evaluate everything from the earthly (or worldly) perspective. We think, *Lord, instead of giving us someone weak, mild and humble, how about giving us somebody strong, solid and self-assured?* It is precisely when we have these kinds of thoughts that we should heed Solomon's wisdom, which says, "Trust in the Lord with all thine heart; and lean not unto thine own understanding" (Proverbs 3:5).

How much wisdom does it take to expect strength from the strong or light from the sun or water to be wet? None, obviously.

Those things are logical God-given facts based on His universal laws. Having, therefore, infused these elements with His truth, He then goes about refuting them, rendering them ineffectual by His godly reasoning.

Through David He says He is the strength of my life (Psalm 27:1). Through Paul He says, "When I am weak, then am I strong" (2 Corinthians 12:10). Also He said, "Let there be light," long before there was a sun and moon (Genesis 1:3,14). Yes, and the Word says He set the water at naught (2 Kings 2:19) and healed these waters (2 Kings 2:21) by dumping salt in them. Everyone knows salt water makes a terrible drink.

The children of Israel went through the midst of the sea on dry ground (Exodus 14). Without so much as a puddle, Lord? And do you know whether Jesus got wet when He walked on the sea (Matthew 14:26)? I choose to think not, if only because He could open the sea for five miles and after only twelve hours (or less) cause more than two million people to cross over the sea bottom on dry ground (Exodus 14:22; Psalm 66:6). Do you see the implication of that? Can you envision how it would be possible for the ground to be totally dry in so short a time? That's God! That's Jesus! That's the Holy Spirit!

And here is the *kicker*: That very same force that set the earth in motion; that same power that opened the windows of heaven and broke up the fountains of the great deep (Genesis 7:11); that same energy that opened the Red Sea; that very same irresistible surge that *raised Jesus from the dead*--all of that is resident in you and me!

What does all this prove? And how is your healing related to these seemingly world-shaking events? I say this: these enormous occurrences and forces are not in the Bible to fill up space. They are there to show you the awesome power of God, to let you see that He has control of everything His grace is able to penetrate when it is given over to Him--even to the pulling down of the stronghold of your unbelief.

There are some teachers today who would have you believe that you are saved *through* faith, but that isn't what the Bible tells us. It says, "By *grace* are ye saved through faith" (Ephesians 2:8) So we see that though *faith* plays a part, it is God's glorious *grace* that gets the job done. He set the pattern and gave us all the criteria for being *saved*, which, in the Greek, is *sozo*, whose precious meanings should thrill the hearts of you who are seeking health and wholeness. For by the very act of being saved or having "a salvation experience," one receives healing, health, wholeness and preservation as part of the transaction. Best of all, one receives an active Savior whose love is boundless and whose grace is limitless. Can you see yourself as the sheep of His pasture in the 23rd Psalm?

There will certainly be those who say, "I have been saved for twenty years and I am still sick. How come?" I have no idea what that statement expects to prove unless they are saying, "Well, God has certainly failed in *my* case." Since the Bible says that God cannot possibly fail (Deuteronomy 31:6), I wonder if you ever entered fully into His grace. You can, you know. It is just a matter of *doing it*. Like your brain, your heart or your left nostril, His grace goes everywhere you go, only you do have to be conscious of HIs grace in order for it to work at peak efficiency. Another thing you must know: if His grace didn't surround you at all times, the devil would kill you in a heartbeat. As it is God's will for you to be healthy and whole, it is Satan's purpose to deceive and, therefore, to kill you.

Entering into God's grace is like entering into a love affair with someone you are greatly desirous of pleasing. Only instead of the love affair being with a member of the opposite sex, it is with God, our heavenly Father, the ever-existing One, the all-sufficient One, El Shaddai, the One who is more than enough, ad infinitum. By His *grace* we enter into the salvation experience and therefore the kingdom of heaven, where there is no such thing as an incurable disease or a terminal illness.

For you who have never entered into this dimension in God and would like to, you might say this simple prayer:

Heavenly Father, in the Name of Jesus, I come before You as a
sinner. And Father, I repent of my sin and turn back to You. I ask
You to forgive me for being so long coming to this day and hour,
this time of decision. Now, Lord Jesus, I ask You to come into
my heart and to be my personal Lord and Savior.

Amen--and Amen

If you said that prayer, I urge you to understand that Satan is just as
real as you are, despite the fact you can't see him with your physical
eyes. Keep in mind that one of his primary goals is to deceive you
and rob you of your rights in Christ. Also remember this: regardless
of what you think, how you feel or what you see or hear, when you
invited Jesus to come into your heart, *He came*, because that is what
His Word says. It also says, "Lo, I am with you alway, even unto the
end of the world" (Matthew 28:20).

It shouldn't be difficult for you to see that most of us need the
renewing of our minds (Romans 12:2), because too many afflicted
Christians are crying out to God to do what He has already done.
Why? Because they haven't the foggiest notion how to enter into the
sufficiency of His grace.

Where God promises in numbers of places, "I will never *fail*
thee, nor forsake thee," and "I will never *leave* thee, nor forsake thee"
(Hebrews 13:5) and "Lo, I am with you alway, even unto the end of
the world" (Matthew 28:20), people somehow can't grasp the reality
of those promises when they have sickness or pain in their bodies.
The presence of pain seems to overshadow God's presence: they can
easily *feel* the presence of pain; they can't as easily *feel* God.

Therein lies the trap: *"I can feel it, so it must be real."* Does that
mean God is not real because you can't *feel* Him? Think how that
must grieve the Lord God, Jehovah Rapha, who said, "I *am* the Lord
that healeth thee" (Exodus 15:26b).

The Hebrew word *rapha* is interesting indeed. In essence, it
means, "I *am* your healing; I *am* your health; I *am* your wholeness; I
am your physician." Almost no one reading this book can say he has

not seen the evidence of this, one way or another. Who of us hasn't had a cut or bruise and watched it disappear? How is that done? And is it not a graphic illustration of the presence of God in our bodies? And what of the principles involved? Well, without so much as a *by your leave*, healing comes. Why? Because the Lord has already said, "I *am* your health; I *am* your wholeness."

That being so with small cuts, burns and bruises, what about the big stuff--the things that are considered terminal and/or incurable? There is a charming if obvious answer. The Word doesn't say, "I *am* the Lord that healeth thee--except when it is serious, terminal or incurable or when the doctor has said you have only a few months to live."

Did you grab hold of that? Well, for goodness' sake, don't let go! There is much, much more.

Bring thy son thither
Read Matthew 17:14-21; Mark 9:14-29; Luke 9:37-43

"Bring thy son thither," Jesus said to the father of the epileptic boy when He came down from the Mount of Transfiguration. The man besought Jesus to heal his son, explaining that His disciples had failed to cast out the dumb spirit which had plagued his child for so long. The Lord then bemoans the fact, saying, "O faithless and perverse generation, how long shall I be with you, and suffer you? Bring thy son thither." And when the boy is brought forth, we see a very important revelation unfold.

When the spirit saw Jesus, the Word says, "straightway the spirit tare him [the young boy]; and he fell on the ground, and wallowed foaming." Most of us who have had any experience in the deliverance ministry would have been hustling and bustling around, doing our thing. But not Jesus; He had complete understanding of the problem.

Here is the child, wallowing in the dirt and foaming at the mouth, and Jesus asks the father (quite casually, I feel) what seems an irrelevant question: "How long is it ago since this came unto Him?"

Now, you know the Lord knew how long the boy had been tormented. Why didn't He just jump into the fray and scurry about, shouting excitedly, "My goodness gracious! What a problem!"

Well, in the first place, He didn't *have* a problem, nor did He have any reason for haste. He knew the child had been this way many years and that a few more moments wouldn't make any difference. He knew the child would be set free, because a number of times He said, "Therefore am I sent."

In the second place, Jesus knew the father needed his unbelief corrected. He also knew the importance of diverting the thoughts of the father, whose personal anguish could keep the boy from the deliverance he needed. After the father's explanation about the spirit and how it had tried to destroy the child, Jesus said, "If thou canst believe, all things are possible to him that believeth." In answer, we see the father cry out, with tears, "Lord, I believe; help thou mine unbelief."

After the Lord had accomplished His purposes in the father, He rebuked the foul spirit and it came out of the boy.

Do you see that Jesus knew the need? And can you understand He knows your need more clearly than you possibly can?

Regardless of your answer to this question, not only does He know and fully understand your need but He knows the root cause that keeps you in bondage. Thus, if you will cooperate with His superlative grace, divine health is yours.

Were there not ten cleansed?

Read Matthew 8:1-4; Mark 1:40-44; Luke 4:38-41; 17:11-19

As Jesus is en route to Jerusalem by way of Samaria and Galilee, He is met by "ten men that were lepers, which stood afar off: and they lifted up their voices, and said, Jesus, Master, have mercy on us." These men didn't have any problem understanding they had a need. They knew the need was for *mercy*, which is the outgrowth of God's love, with a dash of grace and a pinch of favor. For we see at the end of the 23rd Psalm, after David's loving confession of God's grace, that *goodness* and *mercy* followed. And we see that, not only did the lepers know their need; Jesus knew their need, as well. The difference, of course, was that Jesus knew how to satisfy that need and the longing of their hearts.

But how did they know it was possible to be cleansed? Had they heard about the leper who came to Jesus, the one who had been made clean before an entire multitude, the one to whom Jesus had given specific instructions to tell no man? (See Matthew 8:1-4.)

Where is the logic here? Jesus is ministering cleansing to a leper in front of an entire multitude and instructs him to tell no one. How could something as dynamic as that be kept a secret, especially when the cleansing was performed in front of a multitude?

The imperative here is that we know and understand the Lord is not foolish: He knew what must happen for the greatest good of the leper. That leper needed to go and show himself to the priest and offer the gift Moses commanded. That was the first priority, because Jesus was acting in His role as Prophet (read 2 Kings 5, concerning Naaman and Elisha). And people of that day would understand those instructions, for they were living under the law of Moses.

To fully understand where I am headed, it is necessary that you visualize the circumstances surrounding this cleansing. Leprosy is a deadly disease, in which parts of the body rot away and fall off or disintegrate. In light of this, you can easily understand why Jesus wouldn't want this fellow rushing off, in the flush of excitement at being cleansed, to tell the world the good news.

Where a phenomenon of this magnitude can be one of the most glorious and precious moments of a person's life, it can also be one of the most fragile. Satan knows if you can keep your healing (or, in this case, cleansing), you will forever be a witness to his defeat in your life.

Using as our example the leper, who has one ear missing and part of his nose, imagine the following scene. An old friend who has known the leper for years and has seen the slow, painful deterioration looks up and sees the leper rushing toward him in a state of great excitement, yelling and leaping for joy. The leper then stops before his friend and stands in an attitude of great triumph. He announces, "God has just healed me!"

Well, that friend looks at the still-missing ear and nose (immediately becoming Satan's friendly tool) and says, "You sure don't *look* healed. Tell me, if your ear and part of your nose is still missing, how do you figure you're healed?"

It is easy to see the problem here. Not only was the man disobedient to the Master's instructions, but he also wholly lacked understanding. Yet he knew he was cleansed. In our healing ministry, we have often seen people obviously healed immediately while others, who knew in their hearts they were healed, had to wait hours, days or even weeks for the manifestation.

In the meantime, while they waited, God was always working all things together for good.

A woman was brought into the prayer room one Friday evening. Her two sons and sister all but carried her in. It was immediately obvious she was in excruciating pain, the kind of pain that goes beyond pain, with a tumor in her stomach the size of a basketball. It made her look nine months pregnant and she wore the mask of death. The doctor had told her sister the woman wouldn't live out the week. So she had called the Department of the Army to ask permission for the woman's sons to come home from Viet Nam to bury their mother.

As God would have it, by His sovereign grace He had let the family know about the miracles happening in the prayer room. I don't know who told them or how they found out. But with the attitude of trying anything, they brought her. It was wonderfully apparent by the way they treated her with tender concern that all of them loved her very much.

Because of our understanding of the healing and health promised in the atonement--and one of our co-workers having dis-

cerned that the family needed salvation--I asked if they had ever
received Jesus as Savior. When they acknowledged they hadn't, I
then asked if they were willing to receive Him, to which they all said
yes.

So there would be no possible hindrance to their prayers, I
rebuked the pain and commanded it to leave. Wide-eyed with astonishment, the woman broke forth with a glorious smile and said,
almost shyly, "It is gone."

With that, I led them all in the prayer of salvation, laid hands
on her for complete healing and rejoiced with them, believing it was
done, in Jesus' Name.

The sister who had been weeping with joy then asked, "Do you
think the Lord would heal *me*? I have had a bleeding ulcer for
years."

I countered her question with a question of my own: "Do you
believe God plays favorites? Does He love you any less than He
loves your sister?" To which she joyously answered no. Then the
Lord had me ask her about her diet. She responded that she could
eat only the most bland food. Next I asked if she was willing to trust
the Lord completely. She nodded somewhat hesitantly, at which
point I asked if she had a steak in her freezer at home. She said she
did. Then I said, "Here is what I want you to do. I want you to go
home, take the steak out of the freezer, put a lot of salt and pepper
on it, fry it in some vegetable oil and eat all of it. Are you willing to
do that?"

"It might be painful," she responded, "but *I will do it*."

Laying hands on her in the Name of Jesus, I rebuked the ulcer
and commanded it to dry up from the root (Mark 11:12-21). Then
they left, rejoicing!

Now if those two women had rushed out to see their doctors, to
tell them of their healing, they might have been discouraged by such
words as, "We know miracles still happen, but it is seldom, so you
better let me examine you." Doubt would immediately enter in,

along with wondering in their hearts, and the whole thing could have been down the tube.

But that wasn't what happened in this case. Six months later, the sister who had had the ulcer rushed up to me and said, "That was the best steak I have ever eaten!" before I recognized who she was. Right behind her was a woman I didn't recognize at all. Slim and beautifully at peace, she was the other sister, who told me the giant tumor had taken just two months to disappear. My heart nearly burst with joy. I don't know whether it was for her, for Him or both. But I knew it was thrilling.

Now back to Matthew. It is my personal belief that he did what Jesus told him to do. The ten lepers in Luke also had the confidence not only to ask but to receive Jesus' instructions and be instantly obedient.

There is one other element not yet addressed in this case: the grateful heart, the means by which we can show the Lord our appreciation for His grace, goodness and mercy. After Jesus said to the lepers, "Go shew yourselves unto the priests," as they went, they were cleansed. Then the Word goes on to say, "And one of them, when he saw he was *healed*, turned back, and with a loud voice *glorified God*."

Thus, this revelation: when he turned about and glorified God, falling at Jesus' feet, giving Him thanks, the Lord marveled and said, "Were there not *ten* cleansed? But where are the nine? There are not found that returned to give glory to God, save this stranger [who was a Samaritan]. And He said unto him, Arise, go thy way: thy faith hath made thee *whole*." He was not just cleansed, which is pretty big stuff in itself; he was made *whole*, totally restored in every area of his life--spirit, soul and body.

Do you wish to be every whit whole? If that is indeed your heart's desire, have you been giving glory to God *in the midst* of your affliction? Not *for* your affliction, mind you, but in the midst of whatever is your personal trial? If not, you might wish to address the issue with a prayer such as this:

*Heavenly Father, I give You praise, honor and glory, for in You I
live and move and have my being. And Father, since You are
great and merciful and the only true God, possessor of heaven
and earth, I come before You in prayer and supplication, with
thanksgiving in my heart, for the splendid things You have set
aside for me from the foundation of the world. And now, Holy
Father, I call unto You, for Your Word says that when I do, You
will answer me and show me great and mighty things I can't even
imagine. Along with such a promise, Father, there is certainly
health and wholeness, for which I thank You, in the Name of
Jesus Christ of Nazareth.*   *Amen--and Amen*

And He touched his ear
Read Luke 22:50,51

Think of the confusion there in the Garden of Gethsemane. The soldiers had surrounded the place, their torches hissing and sputtering,
the disciples astonished and in complete disarray, the normal serenity of the place wholly shattered by the orders of the guards. Then
poor Judas, in the midst of all this, attempts to casually come up and
kiss Jesus, that being his signal to those who had perhaps never seen
Him.

It is here that we see the Lord in one of His more formidable
roles, that of the sweet innocent. He asks Judas, "Betrayest thou the
Son of man with a kiss?"

Look at the ensuing scene: one part of the guard trying to
round up the disciples; the main body seeing that Jesus didn't escape; the disciples dodging about thither and yon, seeking a route of
flight; Judas kissing the Lord and saying, "Master, Master"; Jesus asking, "Whom seek ye?" (as though He didn't know); the guards answering, "Jesus of Nazareth"; Jesus saying, "I am He"; the guards falling to the ground under the power (John 18:6)--

In the midst of all that mayhem, chaos and confusion, when
Peter drew his sword and cut off Malchus' ear, we see the unparalleled calm of the Lord. Not the smallest detail escapes His attention.

In the midst of this maelstrom, knowing what was about to follow for Himself, Jesus touched Malchus' ear and healed him.

Can you imagine such calm, such unselfish thinking of others instead of Himself, such absolute presence of mind?

I must work the works
Read John 6:28-33

"I must work the works of Him that sent Me," Jesus said, concluding with the words, "while it is day: the night cometh, when no man can work" (John 9:4). We know it was the heavenly Father who *sent* Jesus. But when is it *day*, and when will the *night* come when we will not be able to work? Do you know? No? Well, neither do I for certain. But I sure know what the works are.

They are all a part of God's infinite grace, the blessings we cannot possibly merit, the favor we cannot possibly earn. Jesus said we are to preach the gospel to every creature (Mark 16:15), or by whatever means, see that it is preached, for that is one of the ways the grace of God will be expanded and perpetuated. By so doing, we will be able to heal the sick, cleanse the lepers, raise the dead and cast out devils as demonstrations of how the Word works the works. But, you might ask, "How did I get into the act? I thought the Bible said *Jesus* was to do the works of God." It does, of course. If, however, that is the sum and substance of your query, it is obvious you have never made an in-depth study of *toolship*, which is so far-reaching in its scope it fairly boggles the mind.

There are two all-important qualifications for the course in toolship. One, the student must be able to instantly recognize the difference between the tool and the craftsman; and two, he must be absolutely certain which of the two performs what service.

To begin with, the most basic fundamentals are these: it is imperative we realize that Jesus is the Master Craftsman and we are the tools--if somewhat rusty, dull, bent and improperly sized. We must also realize there will be many tools that are (and will remain) unusable, because that is either how they choose to be or else they

don't know how to make themselves available to the Master. But for
those who wish to become tools of craftsman-level excellence and efficiency, we must know our capabilities and limitations. Though the
Words says, "I can do all things through Christ which strengtheneth
me" (Philippians 4:13), it would be foolishness for the hammer to try
to act as a screwdriver or vice versa. For as the screwdriver is a
wondrously simple tool for anchoring screws, and the hammer is
great for driving nails, they are not interchangeable in their use.

What is this *toolship* analogy setting forth? It is simply saying,
"Be who and what God made *you* to become. Then you will fit perfectly into the hand of the Master and do great and mighty works
which thou knowest not."

At Capernaum, the people came to Jesus and asked, "What
shall we do, that we might work the works of God?" Knowing their
hearts and where they were headed, Jesus gave them one of His typi-
cally pointed answers: "This is the work of God, that ye believe on
Him whom He has sent." That was heart-wrenching stuff, especially
in the light of their next question. For after seeing Jesus perform
mind-blowing miracles of every type and description, they had the
audacity to ask, "What sign shewest thou then, that we may see, and
believe thee? what dost thou work?"

Then, as they continue, you can almost read the sneer: "Our
fathers did eat manna in the desert; as it is written, He gave us bread
to eat," as though to say, "Let's see You top that."

But the Lord Jesus was never guilty of having *an* answer, nor
one of many. He always had *the* answer, which said it all: "Jesus said
unto them, Verily, verily, I say unto you, Moses gave you not that
bread from heaven; but My Father giveth you [and here He speaks
of Himself as the bread of life] *the true bread from heaven*. For the
bread of God is He which cometh down from heaven, and giveth life
unto the world." That world is you and I, people. He *gives life* to us.

We know Jesus said of Himself that He is the way, the truth
and the life and that no man comes to the Father, but by Him. Also
the Word says that He brought *grace and truth*, among the major

blessings of which are certainly healing, health and wholeness, which Jesus describes as the children's bread (Matthew 15:21-28). So "Take and eat," He said. It was His body that was offered for us.

You might pray softly,

Lord God, Your Word says You have made all grace abound toward me. And I ask You by Your Holy Spirit to show me step by step the things I can do to be wholly immersed in Your channel of blessings. I know Your Word says that I have been healed. But in my humanness I don't fully comprehend all the intricacies of health and wholeness as they relate to my body. So Father, I invoke the Name of Jesus and ask that Your grace, goodness and mercy be made so real to me that I will be able to hold and fondle them and have plenty to give to others in need. I know that grace is one of the good and perfect gifts that Your Word says come down from the Father of lights, "with whom is no variableness, neither shadow of turning" [James 1:17]. So now, Father, I appropriate the gift of grace, in the Name of Jesus, and call the healing of my body done.   *Amen--and Amen*

Finally, beloved, it should be apparent that the few examples of grace recorded above are barely surface scratchers. However, for those in need of a touch from the Lord, they are a pretty good beginning. Amen?

2

Healing, Health and Wholeness
By the Laying on of Believers' Hands

These signs shall follow them that believe
Read Mark 16:17,18

Nearly everyone knows about the laying on of hands, but how many of us believe when we lay hands on the sick, they shall recover? Obviously not too many. Yet there are some twenty scriptures that tell us Jesus, Paul and Peter touched or laid hands on the sick: Matthew 8:1-3,14-17; 9:18,19,23-30; 20:30-34; Mark 1:40-42; 6:56; 7:32-35; 8:22-25; 9:17-29, to name but a portion of them. This, of course, doesn't take into account the numberless multitude who followed (or were brought to) Him for healing.

"But," you say, "that was Jesus, the Son of God."

Yes, it was. But wasn't it this same Jesus who said, "And these signs shall follow them that believe in My Name [which should be you and me], . . . they shall lay hands on the sick, and they shall recover" (Mark 16:17,18)?

For you who are wondering about the missing *semicolon* after the word *believe*, it was left out purposely because it didn't exist in the original Greek text. Besides, the full thought here is not "them that believe"--because there are many who believe (whatever you care to name) who will never do anything--but "them that believe in My (Jesus') Name." An intensive study will clearly reveal that not only are we to believe *in Him* but we are to comprehend our rights, authority and privileges--the power of attorney, if you will--that is ours in that Name, the Name of Jesus.

And Jesus put forth His hand
Read Matthew 8:1-4

"And Jesus put forth His hand and touched him, saying, I will; be thou clean, and immediately his leprosy was cleansed." Not only was this a gracious act of love, it also involved the laying on of hands. And not only was it the laying on of hands, it was laying hands on a leper.

How many of us would have the courage to touch a leper under any circumstances? And how many with the courage would have the faith to believe (in the face of such dreadful disfigurement) that the leper would recover?

Your answer is not so important as your meditating on the matter. For in addressing healing by the laying on of hands, it is important that we go back to our brief study on toolship, where we discovered that Jesus is the Craftsman and we are the tools. He masterminds the project and forecasts the ultimate results, while we are merely the elements used to move the task along toward a satisfactory result or glorious conclusion.

Although many pastors and teachers refer to the laying on of hands as a point of contact, it is also an act of loving obedience which God is bound by His Word to honor.

Satan hates the laying on of hands. He will do anything in his power to discourage believers from participating in it. What it does, of course, is punch holes in numbers of his doctrines, such as: healing went out with the apostles; healing is not for everybody; it certainly isn't for today; you don't have to actually *touch* them, you can just sit there and quietly pray; if you don't get sick, how are you ever going to die?

If you have decided to ignore him and go forward to lay on hands or to have hands laid on you, he has devised a number of snares and traps: be sure to wait for a sign; wait till you feel the anointing; feel it and see if it's still there; go to your doctor and have it checked out; if you don't have it x-rayed, it isn't valid, you know; and his old standby, seeing is believing.

But none of these snares and traps have any basis in scripture, especially "seeing is believing." For the Word of God says, "Believe Me and *then* I will show you" (see Mark 11:24). The Word *doesn't* say, "They shall lay hands on the sick and, when they see a sign, or have an anointing, or get a good feeling, or see something spectacular, they shall recover." It says, "They shall lay hands on the sick, and they shall recover," no matter what you see, feel, taste, smell or think.

For you who have never done this because the devil has told you it isn't your ministry or "What if it doesn't work? You'll look like a fool," I can tell you from experience that there are few things more exciting or fulfilling than to lay hands on the sick so they will recover.

One Friday night a woman came into the prayer room and asked us to pray for her. When I asked what she would like us to pray for, she seemed quite reluctant to tell us. When I explained to her it was necessary to seek the Father with specifics rather than with something vague, she told us she had a large cancer in one breast and a tumor in the other. She was to be operated on the following Thursday to remove the cancerous breast and quite possibly the one with the tumor, if investigation showed the tumor was malignant.

When I asked if she would like Jesus to heal her, she said yes. I then agreed with her that He would do it and *laid hands on* her upper chest, commanding that foul cancer and tumor to dry up from the root, after which she thanked us and left.

Ten days later we heard the outcome. Before going to the operating room she demanded to be x-rayed, which threw the hospital into turmoil. Even the doctor was upset and told her the reason they were operating was that they had numerous x-rays already, showing that she had a massive cancer in one bosom and a large tumor in the other.

"But, doctor," she said, "last Friday night, God healed me. No knife is going to touch me until I see some new x-rays."

With much exasperation, the new x-rays were taken. They could find *nothing* in the breast with the cancer. And in the one that had a tumor the size of a pigeon egg, there was a thing the size of a green pea, which, when they removed it, turned out to be benign. "Hallelujah to Jesus!" as Kenneth Hagin might say.

For you who might find things like this either hairy or scary, you can seek the Lord's purpose in this manner:

Father, You, knowing all things, are aware I have never laid hands on the sick. But, Father, it is my heart's desire to be pleasing to You and to do those things Your Word commands. So I ask that, by Your Holy Spirit, You set the circumstances and pattern, so I can overcome my timidity and unbelief, so I can boldly bring before [Your] throne of grace those You have made whole by the laying on of my hands. All this I ask in the Name of Jesus.

Amen--and Amen

Silver and gold have I none
Read Acts 3:1-10

"Silver and gold have I none, but such as I have give I thee; in the Name of Jesus Christ of Nazareth rise up and walk," Peter said. "And he took him by the right hand, and lifted him up: and immediately his feet and ankle bones received strength."

As we know, Peter and John were entering the gate of the temple which is called Beautiful, on their way to afternoon prayer, when they saw a certain man lame from his mother's womb, who was carried daily to the gate to beg or, as the Bible says, to ask alms.

In the introduction to this book, I mentioned that the Lord uses twelve ways to heal His children. Further, I said that there were *ways within ways* as well. Here, though we are still dealing with laying on of hands and touching, there is an excellent example of the ways within ways--four obvious means God uses in the healing process:

1) His grace
2) the Word by command, "in the Name of Jesus Christ of
   Nazareth"
3) the use of hands (Peter taking the man *by the right hand* and
   lifting him up)
4) the obedience (or action) factor

There is another thing that should be seen here: this surely wasn't
the first time Peter and John had passed this way. It is likely they
went to the temple every day they were in Jerusalem. Perhaps even
Jesus passed this way when He came to teach in the temple, which
was often (Luke 22:53). So what happened on this particular day?
What made Peter and John take notice on this occasion? Was it perhaps the grace of God who knows all things, especially *when what*
should occur?

Have you ever seriously considered what really happened at the
Beautiful Gate? How much was accomplished by man? And how
much by God? Do you truly believe God can do anything?

At the risk of seeming irreverent, I must burst a bubble here.
Many people say, "God can do anything," but that simply isn't true.
Though He is certainly *capable* of doing anything, God has so re-
stricted Himself by His Word and by His decision not to violate the
will of man that He sometimes doesn't act. We often accuse Him of
being ineffectual in certain areas we would like to dump on Him.
But most of the time a little attention to His Word will reveal that
these are areas He has turned over to us.

Though we read in three of the Gospels that Jesus said, "With
God all things are *possible*," the word *possible* doesn't mean "likely,
assured, or guaranteed." In the Greek, the word is *dunatos*, which
means "powerful, mighty, strong, capable or able," none of which
imply *guaranteed*. Do you understand that?

What is needful in matters concerning healing is to determine
whose responsibility it is to do what, when and how. It was positively
staggering, during the first months of our ministry, to do something

as simple as lay hands on the sick and see the miracles that followed.
I knew there was just no way--by any personal achievement or physical endeavor--I could lay hands on anyone and have something astonishing happen. Yet astonishing things happened. But there was a
difference between Jesus' ministry and mine: the scriptures say He
felt virtue (or power) go out of Him, but I didn't feel anything. It
would have been a great comfort indeed to feel something, but I
didn't--except on certain evenings, when the healing ministry would
spill over into the morning hours. Then I felt drained.

Of the many hundreds of people the Lord healed, one particularly
precious one was Billy. He had flaming red hair--and he also suffered from epilepsy. Though he had met the Lord and was joyous
most of the time, he didn't understand why his affliction remained.
You see, He expected God to just take it away. But God *seldom*
works that way. Although we have seen Him do great and mighty
things through the Holy Spirit's sovereign intervention, most of the
time it is His good pleasure to work through His people. However,
there is a unique consideration God wishes us to understand: He
doesn't use a lightning bolt to light a twenty-five-watt bulb.

In Billy's case, the Lord wanted it done in the prayer room.
Nevertheless, it was several weeks before Billy came. In the main
meeting, he always sat near Toots and me. He knew about the
prayer room, as we knew about his affliction. But we never tried to
persuade him to come. It would need to be his own decision.

But one night Billy finally appeared. We had just finished praying and there he was--smiling, yet obviously confused. He didn't
believe healing was for him because he had the epilepsy from the
time he was a child (he was now in early manhood). But after we
had agreed together, laid hands on him and rebuked the foul spirit,
Billy found himself gloriously set free. You have never seen anyone
so joyful. For weeks he did little more than laugh. That was Billy, the
laughing one.

Backing up a bit, perhaps I shouldn't have said I never felt any-thing but drained. I most certainly did: quite often I felt foolish. At the time, I was only a two-year-old babe in Christ and I hadn't yet learned how to deal with Satan. When he kept telling me what a simpleton I was and how all this healing business was going to one day come home to roost, I didn't know but what he was right. Yet somehow I knew--really by the Holy Spirit rather than by instinct--that if I was doing what God said to do, I couldn't be all wrong. So I kept laying hands on the sick and patiently waiting for the outcome. And other than the few times I made stupid blunders by trying a new technique or a different approach--leaning heavily on my own under-standing--there were almost no failures.

During those three years in the prayer room I learned some-thing wonderful: since it is impossible for God to fail, if I do precisely what He says to do, it is equally impossible for me to fail.

"If He can't fail," you say, "and you can't fail [oh, but I can], how is it some don't get healed? Who fails and how? And what, if any-thing, can be done about it?"

Although the answer to such questions is not a popular one, it is simple and true: when healing came in, Satan either stole it from you--or you gave it to him. For the Word says, "God anointed Jesus of Nazareth with the Holy Ghost and with power: who went about doing good, and healing *all* that were oppressed of the devil; for God was with Him" (Acts 10:38).

In light of this scripture, could there be another answer? "Jesus Christ (is) the same yesterday, and to day, and for ever" (Hebrews 13:8). God doesn't fail; it is people who fail.

One night a young girl came in on crutches. It was obvious she was not used to them. Two young men had to help her in and seat her. I never learned their relationship, but she was visibly distraught and they seemed greatly concerned. When I asked her need, she said she had been in an automobile accident and, after months of treat-ment, that morning the doctors had told her that she was paralyzed from the waist down and might never walk again.

There it was. And I didn't have the foggiest notion what to do. But isn't it thrilling to know God has the perfect answer. I was just standing there like a lump, wondering what to do, when the Lord dropped the Beautiful Gate incident in my spirit. So I immediately asked her two questions: "Would you like to walk?" to which she answered yes, with eyes swimming, and "Are you willing to walk?" to which she only nodded.

Then, following the leading of the scriptures, I took her by the right hand and lifted her up, saying, "In the Name of Jesus Christ of Nazareth, rise up and walk."

She came up out of that chair with such force I was nearly bowled over. I literally had to jump aside. For a moment she just stood there blinking. But when she looked down and saw she was standing, she started laughing and crying, took off at a brisk clip and walked the block-long corridor twice.

God had performed the miracle two thousand years before at the whipping post in Pontius Pilate's courtyard, and the young girl received it and acted on it that night at Georgetown University.

To illustrate that God doesn't change (Malachi 3:6), that healing (in its fullest consequence) has been given over to man, God gave us a related but very different experience a few weeks later. This time the woman was middle-aged and weighed more than two hundred pounds. Like the young girl, she was on crutches and had to be helped in and out of chairs.

After she told us what was wrong, I asked her the same two questions: "Would you like to walk?" and "Are you willing to walk?" to which she also answered yes. From that point forward, any resemblance to the previous case died aborning. Whereas I could have conceivably lifted the young girl bodily, I couldn't have budged this woman.

As with the young girl, I took this woman by the right hand and commanded, "In the Name of Jesus Christ of Nazareth, rise up and walk." The force of God literally lifted her to her feet full thrust without the slightest help from me. Although she too stood blinking

for a moment, she kept moaning, "No. . . . No. . . . No." Turning to
see where her chair was, she flopped down as though exhausted.

What happened? Who failed--and how? It is my belief that had
she taken that all-important first step, she would have walked as
freely (but for the age difference) as the young girl. However, this
woman is still on crutches, still asking the Lord to heal her. Will she
ever have another such opportunity? I don't know. Certainly our loving Father is willing; He never gives up on us. But whether or not
she will have another opportunity is not the right question. The question is, when she has another opportunity, will she again listen to
Satan--who will surely remind her how God failed the last time--or
will she take that all-important first step?

In circumstances such as this, the following prayer might well
be used:

*Heavenly Father, I ask You by Your Holy Spirit to teach me to
have the discernment--and the sensitivity--I need to minister to
others (as well as myself). As You are aware, Father, there are
nearly as many maladies, afflictions, sicknesses and diseases as
there are sins and transgressions against Your Word. So it is important to us who are still bound by this earth suit (our bodies) to
know how to treat it and with which weapons. Your Word tells us,
"The weapons of our warfare are not carnal, but mighty through
You to the pulling down of strongholds; casting down imaginations and every high thing that exalts itself against the knowledge
of You and bringing into captivity every thought to the obedience
of Christ." I present You my all--so that You can be my all in all.
For I pray in Jesus' precious Name.*   *Amen--and Amen*

And touched He their eyes
Read Matthew 9:27-31; John 9:1-12

There it is again: Jesus touched their eyes (Matthew 9:29). Why do
you suppose He didn't make clay of His spittle and anoint their eyes,
as He did the blind man in John? Was there no clay? Or did He lack

enough spittle for two? Or could it be the Lord knew what each
needed and how His purposes could best be carried out?

In matters of healing, when we ourselves are afflicted, our
needs may differ dramatically while our symptoms are identical. But
that doesn't have anything to do with the result. Our pasts and how
we were brought up are like landscapes on the human spectrum.
Some people are like Kansas, flat, and they resent it to the point of
getting colitis. Others who wind up with colitis are like Colorado,
with great peaks and valleys. Because their afflictions are the same,
should we treat them the same? Or should we consider their back-
grounds and where they came from? And whether or not it runs in
the family? After all, both of them are agitated and both are suffering from the discomfort of inflammation of the colon. However, they
are different people who might very well *receive* differently, even
though the healing of both might be accomplished by the same spiritual methodology.

In a matter of hours, by the laying on of hands and the imparta-
tion of God's peace, a person could be calmed from the unnatural
agitation of the colon, and the body would quickly begin the healing
process. That is how God planned it from the beginning, long before
He told Moses, "I *am* the Lord that healeth thee." And that is the
way *Jehovah Rapha* intends all healing to be accomplished now--by
Him, through His saints (us).

But back to the two seemingly different approaches to healing
the blind, the two in Matthew and the one in John. Although the accounts differ greatly, there were definite areas of similarity. All were
blind; all were healed; and careful examination will show that Jesus
touched all three of them--not only with His hands but with lovingkindness as well.

Come and lay thy hands on her
Read Mark 5:22-24, 35-43

"Come and lay thy hands on her that she may be healed: and *she
shall live*." Those were the words of a distraught father. His name

was Jairus, a ruler of the synagogue, and at that very moment, his only daughter lay dying at his home. He humbled himself by falling at Jesus' feet, beseeching Him to come and lay His hands on her.

It is not difficult to see the importance men of that era placed on the laying on of hands. Not only was it a form of greeting and a bond of friendship, it was an accepted means of blessing as well. However, I haven't found any evidence of it being a part of any healing process before Jesus came out of Nazareth. Yet in just one year, Jairus knew enough of His ministry to ask Him to lay His hands on his dying daughter.

How did he know to ask? And where had he heard about Jesus' healing ministry? There were no newspapers, radios or television newscasters. Throughout the gospels we see the general public-- which would include the disciples on too many occasions--was not much impressed by hearsay evidence. Again I ask how Jairus *knew*. When did he come to that place of wholehearted confidence in the Lord Jesus? We see he was among the very few who came without the negatives, "if thou canst" or "if thou wilt."

Although humbly, Jairus approached the Lord with the same bold assurance we should. That is how He wants us to come to His storehouse of promises--with a clearly defined requisition for our needs and hearts' desires, knowing the merchandise is already on the shelf, marked with our names and waiting to be picked up. If we don't know that healing is the will of God for us and our loved ones, how will we ever be able to come with that Jairus-style boldness and confidence?

Sadly, it is those people who come before the Lord with the faith-crushing, God-grieving expletive, "if it be Thy will," who are forever crying out, yet wondering why they are not healed. The simplest answer to that particular why, of course, is that they are calling God a liar. They are saying, in effect, "Since I don't have time to read the instruction book [the Bible] for myself, why don't You just go ahead and make it work anyhow? I know You can do anything."

There should be no doubt whatsoever. God has already made His will quite clear. Since He has already made every provision for our healing, how could healing be anything *but* His will? Healing for the entire world was prophesied by Isaiah (53:5), fulfilled at the whipping post in Pilate's courtyard and established for all time by Peter with these words: "By whose stripes ye were healed" (1 Peter 2:24).

"Let these sayings sink down in your ears" (Luke 9:44), Jesus said.

To finish the story of Jairus and his confidence: after the incident of the woman with the issue of blood, Jesus accompanied Jairus to his house, put out the minstrels and mourners (so their unbelief could not interfere) and ministered to the now dead child. Then as He took the damsel by the hand, "Straightway the damsel arose, and walked."

Undeniably, all of us--especially those who need healing in our bodies--need the confident boldness of Jairus, so we can be certain to get the Lord wholly involved. Our prayer for the blessing of boldness and confidence toward God might go something like this:

Heavenly Father, I rejoice to come before You in the Name of Jesus, for I have a request, the granting of which I know will please Your heart. Father, I ask You by Your Holy Spirit to teach me the things I need to know about the confidence I am to have in You--and the scriptures that will show me the answers to my need. Also, Father, since Your Word says, "Let us therefore come boldly unto Your throne of grace" [Hebrews 4:16], I want to know specifically how to do that. I want never to enter presumptuously if that is possible, having committed some foolish act without repenting and asking Your forgiveness. Now, Holy Father, I thank You I can consider this done because I ask in the Name of Jesus --that most precious of all names.   *Amen--and Amen*

And He put his fingers into his ears
Read Mark 7:31-37

"And He put his fingers into his ears and spit, and *touched* his
tongue." This concerned an incident that happened near Decapolis,
when people brought a deaf man to Jesus. This man also had a
speech impediment. What a spot for the faint-hearted, eh? Imagine
how reluctant we would be to spit and touch someone's tongue or
make clay of our spittle and put it in someone's eyes. "Goodness!" we
would say, "That sounds downright unsanitary." Nevertheless, let's
say you had the courage and the daring: think what awful peer pressure you would be under. How would your fellow Christians regard
such a ministry? "Imagine!" they might say disgustedly, "The ministry
of spitting."

One of the great failings of the church today is that it is so busy
looking on the outward deficiencies of its apostles, prophets, evan-
gelists, pastors and teachers (Ephesians 4:11) that it can't see what
God is doing in and through them. For, beloved, worldwide, the
church is bursting at the seams.

However, if Satan can keep our eyes focused on the short-
comings of the man--rather than on his accomplishments--he will
make the image of that man no greater than his stature or the
amount of hair on his head. Yet that very same man--young or old,
tall or short, fat or thin--in the privacy of his prayer closet can rejoice
the heart of God if, regardless of his image, he knows how to open
the way for God to interact in the affairs of nations, states, cities,
churches, houses--or individual hearts. In fact, few indeed are those
who can make it on their outward appearance alone. Whether Presi-
dent of the United States or skid-row bum, each will be known or
fade into obscurity by his individual achievements.

We see Jesus, the Christ of God, as the all-time great achiever,
the only perfectly successful Man. In just three short years He
showed us the glory and majesty of God (Matthew 17; Mark 9) and
the superlative potential of man (Matthew 10; Mark 3; Luke 9).
These scriptures show His transfiguration from Man to God and

back, and His ordaining of the twelve to preach, heal the sick,
cleanse the lepers, raise the dead and cast out devils.

These are just two of the many reasons we dare not disdain anything Jesus did--nor how He chose to do it. As I have previously
pointed out, He knew precisely what to do and how to do everything
because He was God in the flesh (John 14:7-11).

With regard to those spitting incidents, the important thing is
not whether Jesus spit on the ground or on the same finger with
which He touched the man's tongue or why He made clay of His
spittle and rubbed it in a blind man's eyes. The important thing is the
outcome. For the scriptures assure us the deaf man with the speech
impediment had his "ears . . . opened and his tongue . . . loosed, so
that he spake plain." And when the blind man went to the pool of
Siloam and washed the clay from his eyes, the Word says he "came
seeing" (John 9:7). Hallelujah!

Who can say the deaf man wasn't so fascinated with the spitting
procedure that he forgot his affliction long enough for the Spirit of
God to do what was necessary to bypass his unbelief? And as for
watching Jesus touch his tongue, he had to look cross-eyed to do
that. Then think of the gooey business of having clay in your eyes.
Certainly we would hasten to get them washed out if only to get rid
of the discomfort. We are forced to agree Jesus knew what He was
doing: for *both were healed*.

Beloved, it is far past the time for any negative thoughts and
imaginations of our hearts to have any ascendancy or even relevancy.
When those negatives have anything to do with Jesus and what He
did or didn't do--how, when or where--such thoughts are from the
pit of hell. We should be alert to dismiss them instantly. Certainly we
shouldn't entertain them, for like any unwanted guest, the longer we
entertain them the longer they stay.

Satan would be derelict in his evil devices--and please don't consider his being so--if he didn't cause the spitting incidents to be a possible stumbling block to your view of the outcome. If in any way it is,
there are certain truths you should address. No one joyously receives

a dry kiss in the midst of an intimate embrace; moistened lips are certainly part of the ordered procedure here--yes? And since the Bible
assures us, "There is therefore now no condemnation to them which
are in Christ Jesus" (Romans 8:1), I will definitely not be the one to
condemn you for moistening your lips with saliva. How many of us
that are mature haven't had a baby slobber on us?

But, you might say, that was an innocent little baby. And I'm
forced to say, "No, it isn't. It is a human born under the same
umbrella of sin as you were. And though it hasn't yet had as many
opportunities to sin as you have, it isn't one whit less sinful." Isn't
that remarkable--a tiny thing like that being every bit as sinful as you
at your positive worst?

If this seems incredible, that doesn't make it any less true. If it
weren't true, all we would have to do is to lead an exemplary life and
we would be assured of our heavenly home--which is one of the
many lies of the devil. Bunk, if you will.

But, beloved, for those of you who have ever lost an infant or a
child--through miscarriage, abortion, infant death, sickness or
accident--or have wondered in your hearts about its whereabouts,
there is wonderful news. The God of all comfort, compassion and
mercy has made perfect provision for all children who experience
physical death before they reach the age of choice or accountability.
And they will be in heaven to greet you *in that day.* David, by the
Holy Spirit, knew there was *spiritual life* after *physical death,* and
that he would meet his child in heaven. Jesus said, "I am the *root and
offspring of David,* and the bright and morning star" (Revelation
22:16). Because the Word says that David was "a man after God's
own heart," we can certainly be assured that David is in heaven with
the Father, and that David and the child (his and Bathsheba's) are
rejoicing before the throne.

Before we have our salvation experience we are abject sinners
and Satan is our father, mentor and guide. After we come to the
saving knowledge of Jesus Christ, however, God becomes our Father
and sends His Holy Spirit to be our mentor and guide. Then when

we ask for and receive the *baptism with* and the *infilling of* the Holy Spirit, we enter into the power structure of the living God.

Many readers may resent the thought of Satan being--or having ever been--their father. But please don't take your resentment out on me; I am just telling you what Jesus said (see John 8:44). The reason it is important that we understand this is so we will understand how it is possible we are still alive--which is one of the great revelations God has given us. But most of us don't see it for seeing it.

If, as Jesus assures us, Satan is a liar, a cheat, a thief and a murderer from the beginning (John 8:44)--and since we know him as opposer to everything from God--the ultimate destroyer, who goes about seeking whom he may devour (1 Peter 5:8)--it is vital that you ask yourself, "With such a vicious father, how is it possible I'm still alive?" The answer is, of course, that if it wasn't for the ultimate purposes of God, you wouldn't be. But God--*but God--but God.* . . .

Regarding the protection of little children, Jesus said, "Take heed that ye despise not one of these little ones; for I say unto you, that in heaven their angels do always behold [or stand before] the face of My Father which is in heaven" (Matthew 18:10). As for our condition before we were saved, David gave us the answer by inspiration of the Holy Spirit: "The angel of the Lord encampeth round about them that fear Him, and delivereth them" (Psalm 34:7).

Here we see that the angels assigned to watch over children ever stand in the presence of God, awaiting their assignments to protect or deliver them. Our angels surround us and are overseen by the Angel of the Lord (whom we often find to be Jesus the Son before He came in His role as Savior). "But," you say, "what about all the children who die or are killed? Who failed? Their angels--or God? And what about all the Christians and really good people? What happened there?"

I don't know if it will satisfy you, but I have an answer that satisfies me: "The righteous perisheth, and no man layeth it to heart:

and merciful men are taken away, none considering that the
righteous is taken away from the evil to come" (Isaiah 57:1).

The first week I began getting into the Bible, this verse fairly
leaped out at me. Although I had tried to read the Bible numerous
times before I was saved, the devil showed me how ridiculous most
of the miracles were and I believed him. After all, how can you cross
a body of water without a boat or a bridge? And you don't have to
create a universe with stars and planets to know how impossible that
is, just try to create one live blade of grass. In addition, what I read
seemed little more than fuzzy at best. So I bought the devil's
package.

But when I invited Jesus into my heart--and two weeks later
was baptized in water and with the Holy Spirit--I was truly transformed. Not only could I read and understand the Bible (i.e., most of
it), I somehow knew it was true from cover to cover. In the midst of
grasping that truth, I read and understood Isaiah 57:1 to mean that
while God doesn't kill anyone or anything, there are circumstances
and conditions under which He allows people, animals, plants and
(even) planets to die (or be taken away).

It is in this light that we see Isaiah's portrait of a loving, merciful and omniscient (all-seeing, all-knowing) God, who sees the end
from the beginning; who sees something wretched and grizzly about
to happen to one of His beloved creations--perhaps one who has not
yet elected to come under His protective grace but whose heart He
sees and considers righteous and merciful. What would the most
loving Personality in all the universe do in such a circumstance, especially since the Word says, "God saw every thing that He had made,
and, behold, it was very good" (Genesis 1:31)? Here the word *good*
in Hebrew is *tob*, two of the many meanings of which are "precious"
and "best." Would such a gracious God permit the ultimate disaster,
the most gruesome tragedy, to happen to His precious best? Or
would He be more likely to allow the righteous to perish and the
merciful to be taken away from such a fate? What think ye?

You see, beloved, we have a misconception about death. No matter who you are, where you've been or what you've done, you are going to live forever and ever and ever. The only relevant question is *where*--in heaven or hell? In everlasting joy or in everlasting torment? (See the parable of the rich man and Lazarus in Luke 16:19-31.) True, when your spirit (the real you) leaves your mortal body, it will cease to function and will begin its journey back to dust. But the real you is going somewhere. Whether *up* or *down* is entirely up to you.

Though the Lord God may have created you and me for many reasons, His ultimate purpose is for us to be in everlasting fellowship with Him. He wants to show us Arcturus, Orion and Pleiades (Job 9:9). He wants to introduce us to the living universe--to enable us to hear the morning stars sing again (as in Job 38:7). He wants us to emulate the praises offered by the sun and moon, the stars and the heavens of heavens (Psalm 148:3,4a) and to rejoice with the trees of the fields as they clap their hands (Isaiah 55:12). Having learned all these simple things, we will live in perfect harmony with Him and them.

When we put this revelation together with what His Word says about healing--the method or means He has set up to cure whom of what--then we can joyously come to that place of rest where we say with all confidence, "My God reigns. Therefore, nothing by any means can prevail against us."

As many as touched Him
Read Mark 6:56

"As many as touched Him were made whole." Again we see the woman with the issue of blood saying to herself, "If I may *touch* but His clothes, I shall be whole." Isn't that remarkable? He didn't *touch her*, she didn't *touch Him*, but by merely touching His *clothes*, she was made perfectly whole. That defies human logic, some say. I am forced to counter with, "What does that prove, beloved? And how dare we try to marry God's all-knowledge to human anything, espe-

cially logic? Ridiculous! God is neither mocked nor intimidated by
our lack of understanding."

Nevertheless, these questions invariably arise: "Was it the touching of His clothes that made her whole? Or the faith involved? Or
the decision followed by the appropriate action (which is the ultimate faith, some say)?"

Quite possibly it was none of these or it could have been a combination of all of them--her desire to be healed working in concert
with God's overwhelming compassion. Only the Lord Jesus could
make something so complex so infuriatingly simple. For He said,
"Daughter, thy faith hath made thee whole; go in peace, and be
whole of thy plague."

We know there was no *human logic* involved in any of this. It
was entirely our sovereign God working in perfect harmony with
time and circumstances--a God who, my grandson Shiloh at age five
said, "only does marvelous things."

But while we are on the subject of *logic*--God's and man's--we
must address this: "And God wrought special miracles *by the hands*
of Paul: So that from his body were brought unto the sick handkerchiefs or aprons, and the diseases departed from them, and the evil
spirits went out of them" (Acts 19:11,12). There is no human logic
here either, but we can clearly see the logic of God.

If one doesn't know the Lord, to have some man lay hands on a
pile of handkerchiefs or aprons in order to heal the sick and cast out
demons at a distance is unthinkable. But in God's realm of logic,
think how much more convenient that would be than carrying a human (a sick human at that) over great distances. Since there were no
helicopters or ambulances yet on the scene, God knew it would be
far less cumbersome to inspire special miracles by the hands of Paul
so that handkerchiefs and aprons could be carried to the sick rather
than having the sick carried to Paul. What could be simpler--eh?

But back to the woman with the issue of blood. Why did the
healing take *twelve years* to be made manifest? Did the Lord resent
the fact that she went to the doctors before she came to Him? Of

course not. Did the fact that there was no indication that the woman
had any faith before touching His clothes have any relevance? Was
the Lord waiting for her faith to rise up? Again, of course not. His
loving concern is forever the same and nothing we do (or don't do)
will change it.

But looking at those twelve years from a different perspective, I
can only wonder where the woman's head and heart were all that
time while she "suffered many things of many physicians, and had
spent all that she had, and was nothing bettered, but rather grew
worse." Although the Lord's love and compassion far outweigh all
other considerations, He has shown me numerous times and in every
kind of circumstance that He wants us to come to Him *first*--not
after all the guesswork and evil reports have come to naught; not
after all the experiments and prescriptions have failed; not after your
confidence in God's processes has been undermined by unbelief. He
wants to spare you all the uncertainty and anguish. He wants you to
place your confidence and trust in His all-knowledge so that--wheth-
er your need is spiritual or medical--He will have the necessary
authority (given by you) to guide you through the proper channels to
His ultimate blessings and goals for you. He can't do that just because you are nifty or have a need; He can do it only through your
consent, prayer or desire.

As previously pointed out, Jesus came as an Old Testament
prophet and ministered on earth in that role. Now He is our great
high priest and ministers to our needs from the throne room, at the
right hand of the Majesty on high. There He acts as our advocate (or
lawyer), our intercessor (or intermediary) and our shepherd (guide,
leader and provider). By this, we can see that He represents us on all
levels--legal, spiritual and physical.

The Word says, "Seeing then that we have a great high priest,
that is passed into the heavens, Jesus the Son of God, let us hold fast
our profession [better translated as "confession" in contemporary
English]. For we have not a high priest which cannot be touched with

the feeling of our infirmities: but was in all points tempted like as we are, yet without sin" (Hebrews 4:14,15).

What this is saying is we have a great high priest who, day and night, is pleading our cases and representing our causes; who loves us beyond our wildest imaginations; who personally feels and bears our hurts and afflictions; and who knows we carry them in error. For He carried them from Pilate's whipping post to the cross and from the cross through His experience in hell, finally taking them with Him to the throne room, where He is still experiencing those feelings of infirmity for us.

Beloved, where do you stand with this knowledge? Are you experiencing some afflictions you shouldn't? Do you have burdens He has already agreed to carry for you? Are you wondering in your heart about something to which He has already given you the answer in His Word? And are you mad with God because He hasn't gotten rid of your problem *your way*? He has a scripture concerning that. John the Baptist is in prison, obviously miffed with his Cousin Jesus, who apparently hasn't been to see him. After announcing to all Judaea and Jerusalem that Jesus was the Lamb of God, John sent two of his disciples to ask Jesus if He was the One or should he (John) be on the lookout for another (Matthew 11:3). At which point, Jesus sends him a pretty stiff message--with a really tough conclusion. The Lord tells John's disciples, "Go and shew John *again* those things which ye do hear and see: the blind receive their sight, and the lame walk, the lepers are cleansed, and the deaf hear, the dead are raised up, and the poor have the gospel preached to them. [Then comes the bomb--] *And blessed is he, whosoever shall not be offended in Me*" (Matthew 11:4-6). Are you one of the blessed?

If your answer to any of those questions that directly precede the Matthew quotation is *yes*, then I have an unpopular but very scriptural observation for you. Jesus made this statement: "It is the spirit that quickeneth [that gives life]; the flesh profiteth nothing: *the words I speak unto you, they are spirit, and they are life*. But there are some of you that believe not" (John 6:63,64). So where do you stand with this?

Regardless of your answer, here is a simple prayer you might wish to present before the Lord:

Heavenly Father, in the Name of Jesus, I come before You with praise and adoration and in loving supplication. Father, in my great desire to be pleasing to You--and to be in humble obedience to Your Word--I ask that You show me by Your Holy Spirit all the ways You have provided for me to be an overcomer. I want to know how to use Your Word in combination with the laying on of hands. I wish to bypass any temptation to think my way through to victory in healing, health and wholeness (or whatever). And finally, Father, I wish above all things to be guided and led by Almighty God--El Shaddai--in the only perfect way--which is Your way.   *Amen--and Amen*

3

Healing, Health and Wholeness
Through Faith and Trust in the Living God

According to your faith
Read Matthew 9:27-31

"According to your faith be it unto you," Jesus said to the two blind men. How interesting are the manifold ways the Lord uses in His healing ministry--and how exciting it is to view His unfailing results.

Although there is a broad spectrum of *faith teaching* in a host of big ministries today--and certainly the body of Christ has in-depth needs in this area--the fact is, Jesus spoke of faith only twenty times. On the other hand, Paul mentioned faith a hundred and seventy times. Do we then gather that *faith* was more a doctrine of Paul's than of Jesus'? Just how are we to regard this particular truth?

Here I have a goodie for you.

The Word says, "Without faith it is impossible to please Him [God]" (Hebrews 11:6). And here is one of those precious little revelations the Lord drops on us like dew from heaven, surrounding and saturating us. While Paul teaches, exhorts and admonishes us on the uses and purposes of faith--making it one of his major doctrines --the Lord Jesus didn't go into all that because He knew Himself to be *the manifested faith of God* and He and the Father came to take up residence in *us* (John 14:23). Praise God forever. Isn't that stunning?

In addition, where Paul tended to explain what faith is, what it does and how to use it in our day-to-day life, Jesus was the revealer, the exhibitor, the example. While Paul was struck with the fantastic *power* of faith, Jesus treated faith as if it should be as commonplace as breathing in and breathing out. He proclaimed the inevitability and inexorability of faith--likening it to the many mysterious forces of God in seeds and leaven (Matthew 17:20).

Jesus always seemed either surprised or exasperated when His disciples acted out their fears and doubts. He accused them of having little faith. Yet we are shown numerous glimpses of them--in joining their faith to His--doing some pretty nifty things. Peter walked on the water; all of them participated in the feeding of the five thousand (because each of them had to handle at least five hundred pieces of bread and five hundred pieces of fish); and all of them had to leave homes and businesses to follow Him, believing their families' needs would be met. In this day and time, we wouldn't call it *faith*. We would say, "Those guys are crazy--leaving their families to starve. And who is going to fill out the welfare papers? That took a lot of nerve--or faith."

Nevertheless, we can see by the gospels that the failings of the disciples were indelibly imprinted on their memories, for those stories remain for us till this day.

In light of what Jesus referred to as their *little faith*, think what an impression the centurion made when he said, "Speak the word only" (Matthew 8; Luke 7). Jesus said He had not found so *great faith*, no not in Israel.

So we see it is possible to have *little faith* (fair to middlin') or *great faith*. Yet the Bible assures us we all start out with the identical amount, degree or depth of faith: "According as God hath dealt to every man *the* measure of faith" (Romans 12:3). Note, beloved, it doesn't say, *a* measure, as in *one of many* measures, but *the* measure, as in *the only possible* measure. The one exception is Jesus, who was given the Spirit *without* measure--or as John says of Jesus, "He whom God hath sent speaketh the words of God: for God giveth not the Spirit by measure unto Him" (John 3:34).

It is self-evident that anyone having an unlimited amount of the Holy Spirit would have an unlimited amount of faith. When God said, "Let there be light," Jesus threw the switch and the Holy Spirit provided the power. All that just *could* have created the big bang some scientists would have us believe brought the world into being. But if there was indeed a bang, it was caused by God's power bypassing Satan's limited fuse box.

To further pursue Jesus' uses of faith: one of the illustrations He gives is that if we have faith the size of a mustard seed (which He says is the smallest of all seeds), we could say to the *sycamine tree*, "Be thou plucked up by the root, and be thou planted in the sea: and it should obey you" (Luke 17:6). Think what we could do with faith the size of an avocado seed!

In Mark 11:22, Jesus commands us to have faith in God (the faith of God or the God-kind of faith). Certainly if it weren't a possibility, Jesus would never command us to have it, would He? Yet after He had stilled the storm, He asked His disciples, "Why are ye so fearful? how is it that ye have *no faith*?" (Mark 4:40).

In just these few examples, you can see that faith has many facets, many levels of accomplishment and is only perfectly identifiable by the Lord--or the successful outcome of its use.

Thy faith hath saved thee
Read Luke 18:35-43

Jesus told two blind men, "According to your faith be it unto you" (Matthew 9:29). He said to another blind man, "Receive thy sight: thy faith hath saved thee."

Aha! Another of those enigmas. The two blind men in Matthew had to be *touched* and *exhorted* concerning their faith for their eyes to be opened, while the one blind man without being either touched or exhorted was commanded, "Receive thy sight: *thy faith hath saved thee.*"

Why the difference, do you suppose? Was it that Jesus dealt with each according to his needs? But since all three were blind, how did their needs differ? And while we are about it, what a *coincidence* that the needs of the two blind men were identical. How do you suppose Jesus got them together in the same place at the same time with the same need? Nifty, eh?

Study and meditation on healing will usually bring forth a cluster of inter-related facts. In these cases, the same Greek word for *faith* is used in both instances--*pistis*, meaning "faith, assurance, belief, fidelity"--but only the one blind man needed to be *saved*--the Greek word here being *sozo*, which means "heal, make whole, preserve, etc."

The use of these words in the two examples brings forth an interesting conjecture. After *touching* the two blind men, telling them, "According to your faith be it unto you," was Jesus saying, in effect, "Now that I have touched you, if you will use your faith, you can have your sight"? And in the case of the one man, was He saying, "Receive your sight: because I have already discerned that your faith has healed you and made you whole"?

Though these questions are interesting, we are not seeking an answer. Speculation of this sort reveals man at his worst: trying to figure out God and therefore trying to make himself equal with God.

In matters of faith, beloved, it is not so much what you understand about it and how to use it as it is knowing that God has given you enough faith to move mountains or to stop the angel of death in his tracks. Too many people would place others in bondage by saying or implying, "The reason you weren't healed was you didn't have enough faith," or "You didn't put it to work," or some equally silly reason. Nonsense. Don't believe such rot. God gave you every last dram of faith you will ever need.

If all healing could be conquered by faith alone, there would be no sickness in the world. The faith that God has given to us is sufficient to drive sickness and affliction off the face of the earth. God, our heavenly Father, wouldn't declare that He is the Lord that healeth thee and then not give you enough of what is needed to get the job done. He is the very essence of *lovingkindness*, so He could never be guilty of any form of duplicity. Where, then, does that leave us with faith and healing? The answer that best suits my needs is that if

faith could do it alone, the Lord wouldn't have used eleven other
ways. So . . . how about a little prayer on the godly use of faith?

> *Heavenly Father, I thank You that You have given me every bit of*
> *faith I need to move mountains, live in divine health and have*
> *my every need taken care of, so that my family and I have no*
> *lack. It is my unalterable confession that all my needs are met*
> *and I live in divine health and abundance. Yet Father, though*
> *Your Word says faith is* substance, *I know of no man to whom*
> *faith is not mostly a mystery. By Your Holy Spirit, I ask for the*
> *kind of teaching that will make it as clear and as real as the word*
> substance *implies. And though I know the disciples asked the*
> *Lord Jesus to increase their faith and I know what His answer*
> *was, I know I have enough faith for whatever You require of me: I*
> *merely want to know how to* use *faith with godly wisdom, knowl-*
> *edge and understanding, that I may be wholly pleasing to You in*
> *all that I do. In the Name of Jesus.   Amen--and Amen*

Have faith in God
Read Mark 11:22

"Have faith in God," Jesus said. That is the same as saying, "Have the
faithfulness--or the steadfastness--of God. Scholars say it also means
"Have the faith of God" or "Have the God-kind of faith," but I have
never been able to track this down to my personal satisfaction--ei-
ther through the varied translations, the original Greek or back
through the Greek to the possibility of its origin being in the
Hebrew. Regardless of all that, by far the most easily understood
definition of faith is in Webster's dictionary: "trust in God." How is
that for succinct. That says it all, doesn't it?

Many have difficulty with faith because they want to read too
much into it. They tend to make it a mystery that has no possible
solution, something to stand in awe of, like watching a 747 take off.
But we shouldn't regard faith in a way different from how we regard
the breath of life, our heartbeat or the fact we have a brain. Unless

there is some difficulty, we breathe right on. And if our heart doesn't give us trouble, we rarely give it any thought. As for our brain, we are pretty sure we have one--but how many of us have ever seen it?

If, then, our faith is to be regarded as an on-going *force*, how are we to use it in the midst of our afflictions? Is there some special way, some methodology, a book of instructions we can get? I am glad you asked that. The answer is "Read your Bible, pray and trust God."

If that seems an over-simplification, let me explain. Our faith is very much like a muscle: if we use it consistently, it grows strong; if we don't, it becomes weak. If we use it properly, it develops into something splendid; if we use it incorrectly, it can become strained and useless. Why? Because that is the nature of muscles--and faith. That is the way God set it up from the beginning and that is the way it works. The principal difference is that when faith is properly used under the guidance of the Holy Spirit it isn't just splendid, it is *glorious*.

It is knowing this in your heart (not your head) that will strengthen you in faith and trust. You begin to see with your heart (i.e., your spirit or inner man) that cuts, bruises, warts, pimples, blemishes and infections, given time--without any outside help--will virtually disappear seemingly of their own accord. However, we know they are done away by the natural forces built into the human body by God. For those who don't read the Bible, those whose whole dependency rests on their human understanding, I thank God for His goodness and mercy in providing the world with doctors, medicines and hospitals.

Another simple prayer here might be helpful:

Lord God, I thank You for always hearing my prayers and sup-plications when I want to know more about You and Your ways. This day I want to know how to use my faith for myself and for others. I want to know how to set aside the cares and demands of my flesh so I can wholly trust in You and Your Word. I want to

*know how to deal with the fears that attempt to beset me, how to
cast the burden of them on You. And Father, since the Lord Jesus
is the way, the truth and the life, it is my confession that I come
before Your throne of grace boldly, with the full force of faith
working in my life, because of the Name of Jesus and what He
has done for me.*   *Amen--and Amen*

Go thy way; thy son liveth
Read John 4:46-54

"Go thy way; thy son liveth." So said the Lord Jesus to the nobleman
whose son was sick at Capernaum. This man heard that Jesus had
recently come out of Judaea and "went unto Him, and besought Him
that He would come down and heal his son: for he was at the point
of death."

Here we see another dimension in faith about to unfold, one
that is so precious it makes your heart ache for the love God is so
desirous of showing. The nobleman has already confessed his son
was at the point of death, thus unwittingly placing the child under the
dominion of death, hell and the grave (because the Word clearly tells
us *we get what we say*). So it was necessary that the Lord change the
nobleman's confession, that the curse be crushed and faith prevail.
Therefore He challenged him with what would seem a very callous
statement: "Except ye see signs and wonders, ye will not believe." But
the man persisted (as we *must*, beloved), persistence being vital to
dynamic faith (see the story of the Syrophoenician woman's daughter
in Mark 7:25-30). Instead of giving up and going off defeated, he
said, "Sir, come down ere my child die." Jesus then tells him, "Go thy
way; thy son liveth."

With the fundamentals behind us, we come to the finished act
of faith--the act that acknowledges the finished work of Christ before
it is seen with the physical eyes. For the Word says, "And the man
believed the word that Jesus had spoken unto him, *and he went his
way.*" You see, he didn't rush back to Capernaum to see if the word
was true; the Word says he went his way, i.e., he went on about his

business. This was not the act of an unfeeling father: we have already seen that he cared deeply. What this shows us, beloved, is that if you have faith that everything is going well at home, you don't rush home to find out if everything is going well.

It was the next day--after going about his business--that a few of the nobleman's servants met him with the good news, saying, "Thy son liveth." He asked when his son had begun to amend (or recover). When they told him, "He knew that it was at the same hour in which Jesus said unto him, Thy son liveth." The joyous conclusion, of course, was that he himself believed, and his whole house.

One thing that mustn't be lost in the shuffle here is that Jesus never saw the child--nor did He touch him. When the father approached Jesus in Cana, the child was twenty miles away in Capernaum. There is no time or distance in the kingdom. We need have no concern that Jesus is way out there in heaven. For the truth is, He is always close enough to hear your softest whisper (Matthew 28:20).

Where is your faith?
Read Luke 8:22-25; Matthew 8:23-27; Mark 4:36-41

"Where is your faith?" Jesus asked His disciples after He had rebuked the storm. It may be difficult for you to relate these stories to healing and health at first, but kindly bear with me. They are very relevant, as you will see.

The Luke account says, "Now it came to pass on a certain day, that He went into a ship with His disciples: and He said unto them, *Let us go over unto the other side of the lake*. And they launched forth." Kindly note He didn't say, "Let us go *part way across*, for a storm is coming, which will cause you to be fearful. Then to show you I am truly the Son of God, I will rebuke the wind and the raging water and a great calm will follow." No, He didn't say anything like that. He only said, "Let us go over unto the other side of the lake."

Where the Word says, "Behold, there arose a great tempest in the sea" (Matthew 8:24) and "There arose a great storm of wind"

(Mark 4:37), all three of the gospels have Jesus quietly sleeping in
the stern of the ship.

How could He do that? The ship was being tossed about--leap-
ing and plunging in the waves to the point that even these seasoned
fishermen felt they were in jeopardy. So they began to cry out. In
Matthew it was, "Lord save us: we perish." In Mark it was, "Master,
carest Thou not that we perish?" And in Luke they said, "Master,
Master, we perish." All this was done with great fear and anguish,
I'm certain.

The Word doesn't indicate that He was surprised or startled or
immediately went into action. The Jesus I see is absolutely serene,
fully in control, rising to rebuke the storm. All three gospels say, "He
arose and rebuked . . . "

Can you see where I'm headed?

What this says to me is that when there is a great storm or
tempest trying to take over our lives--making us apprehensive, fearful or tormented--the Savior is not far off. We can call to Him and
He will arise. And by His Spirit He will put us in remembrance that
He has given us the authority to rebuke the storm and the raging of
the sea, that He has given us the authority to speak to the situation,
saying, "Peace, be still."

When there is something happening in your body that you don't
know how to handle, you have to first ask yourself the question Jesus
asked His disciples: "Where is your faith?" In whom or in what is
your faith? Is it in your doctor? The prescription medicine? The
hospital? Is it in AT&T because you know you can call for help? The
answer you give yourself could be most important.

Let me here pose a few significant questions for born-again,
Spirit-filled believers:

1. About doctors: Suppose the doctor you are going to for a
   serious consultation (perhaps about an operation) is
   having an adulterous affair, thereby placing himself completely under Satan's dominion. Could you possibly get a

God-inspired answer or opinion from him? There is a remote possibility, of course, but I sure wouldn't want to bet my life on it.

2. About medicine: if this doctor, or even Dr. Straightarrow, wasn't able to make an assured diagnosis, and the prognosis was grim and you were told there was an unproven new wonder drug, would you take it? Not knowing what it does, nor what the side effects might be, could you have confidence in that medicine?

3. About hospitals: in the hospital with all those bottles and tubes and funny little machines beeping at you, with doctors and nurses looking at you like a rotting squash, whispering and nodding and writing mysterious things on charts they won't show you--with all those things quietly shouting, "Boy! You must *really* be in bad shape!" could you honestly say, that you believe the scripture, "*I Am* the Lord that healeth thee" (Exodus 15:26)?

4. About telephones: A telephone is certainly one of the most ingenious inventions God has given man, and certainly there is no more competent industrial giant than AT&T. I would imagine there would be less than one chance in ten million that your telephone wouldn't work in an emergency. It is that efficient. However, AT&T, its subsidiaries, satellites, phenomenal expertise and technology and its stockholders notwithstanding, the Lord is the possessor of heaven and earth, including our great telephone system. So why would you depend on Ma Bell instead of on the Lord? Especially when El Shaddai owns Ma Bell? Not only is He more accessible, you don't have to dial, and He will never send you a bill.

This is not to put down doctors, medicine, hospitals or telephones. And obviously all doctors are not committing adultery or recklessly giving out stupid prescription drugs, but we must be aware of the

enormous gaps in their knowledge of the human anatomy, its functions and built-in regenerative nature. Only God is capable of understanding all that. We must also be aware that no doctor--*no, not
one*--has any power to heal anything. The absolute best he can do is
examine, counsel, prescribe, repair and/or assure. Everything else
has to be left in the capable hands of Almighty God. And we certainly must not let Mother Nature get involved, whoever *she* is.

Again I ask, "Where is your faith? In whom or what?" If your
answer is *God*, then great is your faith indeed, because it is He who
creates it, prescribes its use, supplies it--and then makes it function
at peak performance in and through Jesus Christ the Lord.

"How is it then that so many fail?" you might ask, "that so many
good people and even *innocent little children* die?" I don't know the
answer. What I do know, however, is that God never fails. Also I
know if we wholly trust in Him, we cannot fail either. *He* says so.

How is it that ye have no faith?
Read Mark 4:40

"How is it ye have no faith?" Jesus asked His disciples in the storm
sequence recorded above. These men were His closest friends. Why
did He ask such a seemingly silly question? Certainly He had enough
time to experience the raging of the sea before He rebuked and
calmed it--and He would have known what a fearful thing it was for
them. They didn't have life jackets, rescue equipment or any of the
life-support systems we have today, so if the boat sank, they would
have been forced to swim the three-to-five miles to shore through
the towering waves.

And even if one of them had had the courage to leap to his feet,
grab the mast and shout at the storm, "Peace, be still!" his com-
panions would have thought he had lost his marbles and would have
thrown him overboard. After all, who wants a madman aboard in the
midst of a storm? So where are we? What do you suppose the Lord
had in mind when He asked, "How is it that ye have no faith?"

That must have been a pretty jarring question. The disciples were fishermen and who can imagine men *without faith* fishing for a living, going out in a small boat in all kinds of weather and casting their nets? The only thing more ridiculous would be a farmer planting seed without believing for a harvest.

Why did the Lord ask such a question? Don't you think He knew it was a hairy situation? Of course He did. In the same way, don't you think He knows your problems and concerns and that they are hairy for you? Of course He does.

What He illustrates here is awesome, for He is showing us His power is greater than our storms. He is saying, "When you place your faith, confidence and trust in Me--whether your personal storms are great or small--you will experience a calm assurance that nothing can shake."

This interpretation is borne out in all three gospels: when the Lord rebukes the storm a great calm ensues (Matthew 8:26,27). And His disciples marveled, saying, "What manner of Man is this, that even the winds and the sea obey Him?" Where the men *marveled* in Matthew, Mark says, "They feared exceedingly" (Mark 4:41) and Luke says, "They being afraid wondered" (Luke 8:25). In these few fragments of scripture, we see the same human emotions that surround the fears of illnesses and afflictions, what we think of as "the unknown."

For you who may indeed be suffering some of these torments, I have a few questions for you to seriously ponder:

1) Instead of being terrorized by the storm within, why not *marvel* at Him who gave us authority over it?

2) In place of being tormented by doubts and fears at the raging, why not *exceedingly fear* (or stand in reverent awe of) the One who has taught us how to achieve calm assurance through perfect trust?

3) Rather than giving way to feelings of jeopardy and anguish, why not *wonder in your hearts* at the glorious possibility of

wholeness as we speak to our afflictions with His words,
"Peace, be still"?

Jesus has given us some splendid lessons concerning *peace*. In John,
He tells us, "Peace I leave with you, *My peace I give unto you*: not as
the world giveth, give I unto you" (John 14:27). And in Matthew, the
Lord instructed His disciples, as He was sending them out to minister, "When ye come into a house, salute it. And if the house be worthy, *let your peace come upon it*" (Matthew 10:12,13).

We see that Jesus set great store in the introduction of peace
into most circumstances (see also John 20:19,21,26). The word for
peace in the Greek is *eirene*, which means "peace, quietness, rest,
unity and concord." And I would like to add the word *serenity*, which
comes from trusting in God.

For what are we to trust God? One of the most important
things is to trust Him to hear and answer your prayers. Next, since
one of the principal ingredients of faith is action, it is important to
trust Him to give you a vision of how to interact with His supply.
Finally, trust Him to give you the thrust in your spirit toward a condition of expectancy. Always expect God's best, for it is His heart's
desire to give it to you. Know that your prayers joined to God's love
can give *substance* to what you envision.

Here I interrupt the direction to share a revelation the Lord
just this moment gave me. As I was approaching the last chapter, I
kept getting the word *substance* in my spirit. Though I acknowledged
it, I didn't know what to do with it. "*Substance*, Lord? What about
substance?" When I looked the word up in my *Young's Analytical
Concordance*, my eyes fell immediately on the reference to Hebrews
11:1. And there it was.

Hebrews 11:1 is an exceptionally well-known passage. Even the
most casual Bible student can usually quote it verbatim. So I didn't
regard this as anything more than immediate recognition of that
which is generally known and was therefore about to dismiss it.

In case you don't know, Hebrews 11:1 reads like this: "Now
faith is the substance of things hoped for, the evidence of things not

seen." I had always considered the word *substance* to mean "something envisioned." A thing has to be envisioned, I thought, because how could your faith grab hold of something it had never heard of or seen? Think how difficult it would be to describe an airplane to someone who had never seen one. In my own case, I could best have faith to receive something I had seen and could describe, yes?

I learned from the concordance that the word *substance* goes much further than envisioning or describing. In the Hebrews 11:1 scripture, not only do you have to know the object (or objective), you must know it is upheld, undergirded or supported by a foundation of *hope* (which in the Greek is *elpizo*, meaning "to have hope, hope, hope for--or *trust*"). Isn't that smashing?

Put in the context of building procedure, before you poured the general foundation, if you were on unstable ground, you would put down piers as far as necessary to reach the original earth formation or solid rock. Then the support system would be immovable (or unshakable), as should be our faith and trust in God's promises.

If you are having problems experiencing the peace of God in the midst of the storms of life, you might want to pray this prayer:

Holy Father, I come before You in the Name of Jesus, seeking to fully appropriate the confident knowing of Your peace within me. Your Word says the Lord Jesus left me His peace, so I know it is mine. But, Father, in my humanness, I haven't learned how to use it. I want to use Your wisdom--which You gave me when I asked for it--and Your peace with the same assurance, so that foreign thing in my body can be brought to naught. I thank You, Father, that because I am filled with Your Spirit I can say with all confidence, "I have overcome." In the Name of Jesus.

Amen--and Amen

4

Healing, Health and Wholeness
Through Deliverance
from the Works of Darkness

Get thee behind me, Satan
Read Matthew 16:21-23; Mark 8:31-33

"Get thee behind me, Satan," Jesus said (Matthew 16:23; Mark 8;33; Luke 4:8). In the gospel of Luke, Jesus is telling Satan off when Satan had just offered Him all the kingdoms of the world if He will but fall down and worship him. Jesus said, "Get thee behind Me, Satan: for *it is written*, Thou shalt worship the Lord thy God, and Him only shalt thou serve." But in Matthew and Mark, after telling His disciples about His forthcoming death and resurrection (which none of them understood at the time), the Word says that Peter re- buked Him, saying, in essence, that those things could not happen. Then the Lord turned about and said to Peter, "Get thee behind Me, Satan, for thou savourest not the things that be of God, but those that be of men."

Why did the Lord address Satan, while He was actually speak- ing to (or *at*) Peter? Was it because Satan was using Peter's lips and voice--having first influenced his thoughts--to keep the disciples bogged down in their own confusion and uncertainty?

There is an awful lot we don't know or understand about Satan, fallen angels and demons, isn't there? We are going to do some in- depth exploration of them in this chapter. I want you to know they hate to be exposed to the light.

o don't believe there is a per-
erpent, whatever, nor that
r evil, foul, unclean or deaf
ɡs are real. They do exist.
nce, which was one of the
many instances,
ee.
ws are Satan's minions,
ɛs from the kingdom of
pain, infirmities and vain
urage stress and tear up
ɪs came near one of their
p residence--see Mat-
...υ ρυssessed man saw Jesus, the Word says, "He
cried out, and fell down before Him, and with a loud voice said,
What have I to do with Thee, Jesus, Thou Son of God most high? I
beseech Thee, torment me not" (Luke 8:28). Then Jesus commanded
the unclean spirit to come out of the man (Luke 8:29). This was the
demon leader who said his name was Legion, "because many devils
were entered into the [possessed] man."

This shows us a number of significant things about unclean
spirits:

1) unclean spirits inhabit humans when they can;
2) unclean spirits can speak through their victims;
3) unclean spirits tremble and fall before the authority of Jesus,
   which has been passed on to us. The reason we were able
   to receive that authority legally was that it was given to us
   by the Son of man, not the Son of God (Matthew 10:8).

If you will look in a good concordance under the word *spirits*, you
will find it lists and describes some thirty-two undesirable types--and
dozens of scriptures that tell us how Jesus dealt with them. It doesn't
matter whether they were evil spirits, unclean spirits, foul spirits,

deaf or dumb spirits, all were subject to His words and *He cast them out*. That is hallelujah stuff! The Word says, "God anointed Jesus of Nazareth with the Holy Ghost and with power: who went about *doing good, and healing all* that were oppressed of the devil; for God was with Him" (Acts 10:38).

Jesus went about doing good and setting the captives (of demons) free so we could see the Father was with Him, which brings up a question: Is the Father with you? Do you have any less authority (since Jesus gave you His unalterable power of attorney)? The answer, of course, is no.

God made a plan centered around Jesus and His body (meaning *us*). If, therefore, God is with Him--and Jesus is not disembodied--He can't fail to be with us any more than He can fail at anything else. And His Word says, "And these signs shall follow them that believe in My Name; *they shall cast out devils*" (Mark 16:17).

Why do thoughts arise in your hearts?
Read Luke 24:38

"Why do thoughts arise in your hearts?" A continuation of that question might be, "And where do they come from? Are all your thoughts your own? If not, which are yours and which theirs?"

Spiritual warfare--the war that seems to go on and on in our Christian walk--is one of the most interesting things to study in the Bible. When Jesus asked, "Why are ye troubled? and why do thoughts arise in your hearts?" He had risen from the dead that morning and appeared to Mary Magdalene. Then in the afternoon He had appeared to the two disciples on the road to Emmaus. Now here He was in the early evening appearing to the eleven. They had thought Mary's story an idle tale, and I have no doubt they were skeptical of the two disciples as they told of their encounter on the way to Emmaus. But when He appeared out of thin air right before them, you would have thought they would rejoice, saying, "At last! Now we know the truth."

But that isn't what happened. Even though Jesus greeted them with, "Peace be unto you," the Word says, "They were terrified and affrighted"--can you imagine that?--because they supposed that they had seen a spirit (or a spook). *And after all the times He told them He would come back!*

That is why Paul was so adamant about our being transformed by the renewing of our minds (Romans 12:2). We cannot allow ourselves to be governed by the carnal minds with which we enter into the kingdom of God, for they are subject to every kind of influence--good, evil, whatever--and a lot of questionable stuff in-between.

All bad thoughts are not demon-inspired any more than all good thoughts are God-inspired, but it is incumbent upon us to consider our thoughts (good or bad) and to determine their origin. Unless our minds are blinded by the god of this world, Satan (2 Corinthians 4:4), it is pretty easy to tell. The truth is rarely hidden; what is usually hidden is our resolve to do what we should in the face of opposing forces, whether the world, the flesh or the devil.

It was during one of our first trips after coming to know the Lord that I ran up on a demon spirit. My wife and I had an opportunity to go to Palm Beach for a combination of study, evangelism and vacation. We were having a splendid time, with one miracle after another blazing our trail. But in the midst of all the excitement, a nagging truth began to surface. Something was definitely wrong. I could pick up any secular reading matter--*Time, Life, Look,* whatever--and be bright and alert. But even after a good night's sleep, if I picked the Bible up off the night table, I would instantly begin to doze. "What's happening here, Lord?" I asked, for Toots and I had both begun to notice this unusual phenomenon.

When you put something before the Lord and are truly desirous of having His answer, you may not get the answer you want but you will assuredly get the right one. In my case, the answer was "A spirit."

A few weeks after we met the Lord, Toots and I attended a seminar in Fairfax, Virginia, where Dr. Derek Prince and Don

Basham were teaching on demonology. I didn't know it until I got there nor did the demons, because when someone mentioned *demons,* every demon in me stood up and shrieked. After some good healthy teaching, however, and after seeing numbers of people set free, I knew demons were just as real as I--but a lot more insidious and pervasively active. I determined to unload as much as I could of the graveclothes that had clung to me over my worldly years.

Booze, cigarettes and a host of other junk went pretty quickly but I wasn't yet ready to become what "the others" told me was Mr. Goody Two-Shoes. When we aren't fully committed to serving the Lord, we tend to rationalize what He does and does not really care about, thus leaving ourselves open for every kind of self-deception. And that old serpent just stands there rubbing his hands and chortling, "You give up a little--but you get to keep a lot." But that is only as true as the new believer allows. Jesus defeated the devil for us. That means we are the righteousness of God in Christ (2 Corinthians 5:21) whether we feel like it, look like it, act like it or talk like it. That is true not because that is the way we are in the flesh but because that is the way God sees us. And He says of Himself, "I am the Lord, I change not; therefore ye sons of Jacob are not consumed" (Malachi 3:6).

You can see by that scripture that if His nature and actions depended on our nature and actions, we would already have been consumed, probably at birth. But He is the Lord of the living, the God of love, and He doesn't change.

The levity with which I viewed my activities back in those early days now causes me to shudder. I knew numbers of people who were hung up in adultery and/or fornication who were convinced God wanted them to have a little fun. "After all," their argument went, "He invented it [sex], didn't He?" And though I had by that time pretty well put all that behind me, those little fellows were still working on my human logic in the matter.

I got into all that to show you this: I don't know how I gave the spirit of slumber the authority to interfere with my Bible studies, but

I did. That is how spirits work: they operate only by the authority we give them. How and why are not always clear. But when they knock at your door with some very enticing thought that is neither righteous nor godly, when you answer you have to command them to take their junk elsewhere.

Our role as the righteousness of God in Christ puts us in the position of guardians of our thought life. We cannot afford to have a bunch of little rebel guerrillas sniping at us from their hiding places. It is for us to know their tactics (by reading the Bible) and expose their positions.

That is what happened to the spirit of slumber: we took a bead on his position and knocked him out. We caught him in the act and that always allows us to triumph in Christ Jesus. Because we were able to find him in the scriptures (Isaiah 5:27; Romans 11:8) so we knew who and what we were dealing with, we were able to cast him out in the Name of Jesus.

We could have let thoughts arise in our hearts, i.e., doubt about the existence of demon spirits and what happens when they leave--all that dumb stuff. However, we already knew the author of doubt and fear--the dragon, that old serpent, which is the devil and Satan (Revelation 20:2). Like Jesus, we had commanded him to get behind us. So I was out in the clear. Hallelujah!

God has not given us the spirit of fear
Read 2 Timothy 1:7

"God has not given us the spirit of fear but of power, and of love, and of a sound mind." Are you aware that this truth is given by inspiration of God? (see also 2 Timothy 3:16). All too often we fail to attribute the word *spirit* to a real, living, functioning personality, one whose activities are clearly named in the Word so we will know who they are and how to deal with them.

Some Bible scholars tell us there are 365 scriptures that tell us to fear not, one for each day of the year. I don't care how many times it is said; I only want to know it is either God or Jesus saying it

in the context of a forever-now principle. If we are never to have
fear, not ever, then the love, goodness, mercy and preserving power
of God will be the foundation stone on which we can stand in the
river of life until it is time to launch out and go with the flow.

Many doctors know that more people die from fear than from
the affliction that is causing the fear. Jesus made a statement I consider to be a prophecy concerning our day when He spoke of "signs
in the sun . . . moon . . . stars . . . distress of nations, with perplexity
[neither knowing nor having any understanding of what is happen-
ing] . . . men's hearts failing them for fear, and for looking after
those things" (Luke 21:25,26). . . .

This is not referring to that good, healthy fear--better translated "reverence"--spoken of in Proverbs, which says, "The fear of the
Lord is the beginning of knowledge" (Proverbs 1:7) and "The fear of
the Lord is the beginning of wisdom" (Proverbs 9:10). The *fear* used
in Luke comes from the Greek word *phobos*--the root word for our
word phobia--meaning "fear, terror, dread, aversion." The only good
or healthy thing that can come out of that kind of fear is the knowledge that God didn't give it to us but has shown us numerous examples of how to defeat it. His Word says He has not given us *the*
spirit of fear but all the power necessary to knock it off--either by
renouncing it, repudiating it, or casting it out by the words of our
mouths *with power.*

About three years ago, just after midnight one night, Satan
tried to put a heart attack on me. These were the symptoms: a burning in my chest like a severe attack of indigestion; immediately following that, I suddenly couldn't breathe (or, I should say, get my
breath); after which it felt like someone had dumped a shovel full of
hot coals on my chest; and my right arm ached like a toothache. So I
woke Toots to tell her what was happening. She asked if I thought I
should go to the hospital, to which I answered no.

You see, I had no fear. And I knew Satan doesn't have the
authority to kill me unless I give it to him. I bound the spirit of fear
(Matthew 18:18) to keep him at bay so that Toots and I could con-

fess the Word of God out loud, announcing to all the forces of evil that they were defeated.

Very soon after we began using the Word, we rebuked pain, which soon began to subside. We have full authority to do that--to make the name of pain bow down to the Name of Jesus, and it *must*. The Bible clearly says so: "Wherefore God also hath highly exalted Him [Jesus], and given Him a Name which is above every name: that at the Name of Jesus every knee should bow, of things in heaven, and things in earth, and things under the earth; and that every tongue should confess that Jesus Christ is Lord, to the glory of God the Father" (Philippians 2:9-11).

Here are a few questions to ponder if you doubt our authority over pain. First, is *pain* indeed a name? Of course it is. Second, is it a name of something on the earth? Again, of course. Third, must it bow to the Name of Jesus Christ? Finally, of course.

In my case, not only was the pain forced to bow to Jesus because I used the Word; it also had to leave. For the rest of the symptoms, having no clear word I could directly apply to a heart attack, I fought Satan and all the forces of hell with a number of healing scriptures (included in **Afterword** at the end of this book). At six in the morning, after six hours of battle, I fell asleep. And at ten, I awoke perfectly whole.

Some of you might say, "Since you didn't have a doctor, how do you know it was really a heart attack?"

Call your doctor and read my symptoms to him, as though they were something you are experiencing. If you don't hear an ambulance siren in fifteen minutes, I would recommend you get a new doctor. And for those who might feel that fighting for six hours without knowing you were going to win would be very hairy, I can only say, "If you have any doubts about winning and don't know who your enemy is and how to beat him, you should call the emergency squad with all haste. And you'd better have lots of money or good health insurance. You're going to need them." In my situation, I fought with a Bible I already owned and ten-cents worth of xeroxed scriptures.

As the spirit of fear had no place in Jesus, he has no place in us. He was defeated at Calvary and in hell, along with all the other hosts of the kingdom of darkness. There are none that aren't defeated. And if you are ever fearful beyond having a healthy respect for heights, rattlesnakes and drunken drivers, give the spirit of fear the Word. He absolutely and positively must obey.

A simple positive prayer might be:

Lord God, I thank You, in the Name of Jesus, that You haven't given me the spirit of fear but of power and of love and of a sound mind. Also, Father, that You have given me the power of attorney to use the Name of Jesus. That is awesome, my God. I want to be guided by Your Spirit wherever and whenever it comes time to use that Name. I know that You are with me as You are with Jesus, and that I have been given the same authority as the Lord Jesus to cast out demons, to speak with new tongues, to cleanse the leper, to raise the dead and to heal all who are op- pressed of the devil. Also, Father, Your Word says, "Perfect love casteth out fear" and I know You have given me perfect love and will show me how to use it in the Name of Jesus.

Amen--and Amen

Thou art loosed from thine infirmity
Read Luke 13:10-16

Jesus was teaching in the synagogue on the sabbath, "And, behold, there was a woman which had a spirit of infirmity eighteen years, and was bowed together [or bent over], and in no wise could lift up herself [or straighten up]. And when Jesus saw her, He called her to Him, and said unto her, Woman, thou art loosed from thine infir- mity. And He laid His hands on her: and immediately she was made straight, and glorified God."

As many times as I had read that, I had never noticed before that the woman's infirmity was spirit-controlled. Whether the fact was actually hidden or whether I just didn't see it, I don't know. But the way I found out was sensational.

Five successful businessmen had been singled out by a Jewish reporter for the now defunct *Washington Daily News*. He called me for an appointment, saying that he wanted to do a story on some successful men who were now serving the Lord. Would I consent to the interview? Finding out who the others were and knowing them all personally, I said, "Fine."

He asked a lot of very personal questions, assuring us that our answers would be considered off the record. As it turned out, everything we said should be off the record he put in the article. And most of the things we thought should be printed were deleted. We didn't know whether he or his editor was responsible, but we all felt betrayed, especially a Jewish believer named Sid Roth, whose family didn't yet know about his new belief in Christ.[1]

But God. *But God*. The reporter might have meant the article as a sort of tongue-in-cheek put-down, but the Lord used it for good. While the five of us were murmuring about the report--having our eyes focused on ourselves rather than on what the Lord was doing-- we nearly missed the most important thing. The article wound up on the front page under the blazing headline: NIXON AND CHOU OKAY CHINA-U.S. EXCHANGE. The article itself was captioned "White Collar 'Jesus Freaks,'" with a large photo of yours truly sitting on the corner of my very splendid Louis XVI desk, with my foot casually resting on one of my leopard-covered Regency chairs. Have you got the picture? Dashing, eh? Ugh!

But that wasn't the end of it. First CBN picked up the story-- and a day or two later we got a call from Kathryn Kuhlman's office. Whatever the content, to them the Name of Jesus hitting the front page was really big stuff. And the furor at the paper, with the unprecedented request for copies, threw the *News* into such a tizzy the

----
1. SOMETHING FOR NOTHING, by Sid Roth (Bethesda, MD: Messianic Vision Press, c 1982). Order from Star Books, inc., 408 Pearson Street, Wilson, NC 27893)

publisher in Chicago had difficulty getting a copy. It was so astonishing, reprints were made and sent all over the world. The five of us were stunned.

After we were interviewed on the "700 Club" and on "Charisma," Kathryn Kuhlman invited us to be on her show at CBS in Hollywood.

On finding out our schedule, one of our more prominent charismatic space scientists arranged for me to speak at his church the night before the filming. And that is where I found out about spirits of infirmity firsthand from hearing the testimony of a woman with a prominent healing ministry.

It seems that one day when she was about to lay hands on someone, the person standing next to her said, "Why don't you first cast out the spirit of infirmity?" Just as it had hit her, her words hit me like a concrete truck. Goodness! What a revelation! But, Lord, what do I do about it? Where are they?

As I usually do, when I finished speaking, I asked all those who had physical or spiritual needs to come forward. The Lord sent me twelve people, all with physical needs and all having a spirit of infirmity. There were two with eye problems, two or three with hearing problems, four with bursitis and arthritic symptoms, etc. But the most outstanding case was a man who had back problems. To stop further deterioration to his (spinal) discs, the doctors had fused them together, making flexibility impossible. He sat ramrod straight, and both seating himself and rising to stand were obviously extremely difficult.

After setting the rest of the people free--casting out the spirits with the words of my mouth, watching those with vision problems seeing clearly, those with hearing difficulties hearing keenly and those with physical limitations freely moving their previously afflicted limbs--I asked the man with the fused discs to stand. Then I laid hands on him and said, "You foul spirit of infirmity, I command you in the Name of Jesus to loose this man." Then I said to the man,

"You are loosed from your infirmity. Now bend over and touch your toes."

He looked at me and blinked and said, "I haven't been able to tie my shoes in seven years." I said, quite firmly, "I didn't ask you to tie or untie your shoes. I said bend over and touch your toes."

After looking at me for a few moments--perhaps to make sure I was serious--he murmured something like, "Gracious!" and started bending over, his eyes growing big as saucers. When he touched his toes, he began laughing and straightened up and bent over several more times. He was completely set free.

You can see this is one of the great examples of ways within ways that the Lord uses to heal and make whole. This was not only an example of deliverance, it was also an example of obedience, which we will be dealing with in a later chapter. In the natural, the man had every right to say he didn't believe he could touch his toes, and if he had said it, he wouldn't have been able to do it.

Many people say, "When I broke my wrist [toe, finger, leg, arm, whatever], it was improperly set and didn't grow back straight." Of course, that is possible, but if you are one of those people, don't over-look the possibility that somewhere along the way a spirit of infirmity entered into your situation.

It doesn't matter whether you were or weren't a Christian when it happened, or how long ago it happened, you can still be set free.

We can see from the scripture that the ruler of the synagogue was indignant when the Lord set the woman free on the sabbath, saying, "There are six days in which men ought to work; in them therefore come and be healed, and not on the sabbath day." The Lord Jesus really gave the ruler his comeuppance, saying, "Thou hypocrite, doth not each one of you on the sabbath loose his ox or his ass from the stall, and lead him away to watering? And ought not this women, being a daughter of Abraham, whom Satan hath bound, lo, these eighteen years, be loosed from this bond on the sabbath day?"

There just shouldn't be any doubt: the Lord wants you free. Think of it! Could that woman, bent and afflicted, ever have been a witness to the goodness and mercy of God? Notice it wasn't until she straightened up that the scripture says she glorified God. Can you, with heart-touching conviction, glorify God in your body? (See 1 Corinthians 6:20.)

If you are harboring any doubts as to the reality of the spirit of infirmity and whether he is the author of your affliction, I can tell you he isn't the author (because Satan is), but he could very well be the cause. To be sure, you might well go before the Lord with this prayer:

> *Holy Father, I come to You this day seeking to know the cause of my afflictions. Though Your Word implies that I am to live in divine health, and certainly that is my heart's desire, I am assailed by too many afflictions. No sooner am I rid of one than another is right behind it. I know that isn't either Your will or Your purpose but I don't know where I am failing. Father, I ask You to reveal the cause or causes, whether they are authored by Satan and administered by the spirit of infirmity, or whether there is another cause. And since I know I am Your child, one of Your many beloveds, I also know by Your Spirit that I will be guided to the truth in these matters because I am asking You in the Name of Jesus.*   *Amen--and Amen*

Until seventy times seven
Read Matthew 18:21,22

"Until seventy times seven," was Jesus' answer to Peter when Peter asked the Lord, "How oft shall my brother sin against me, and I forgive him? till seven times? Jesus saith unto him, I say not unto thee, Until seven times: but, Until seventy times seven."

Since, in our ignorance of the Word, we are often guilty of carrying our sin nature into the kingdom with us before our minds are renewed, we are also guilty of taking in some of our graveclothes--

clothes that are still infested with those dark brown uglies from our pasts. What is needful is a spiritual delousing. If this offends you, consider:

I have heard Christians say silly things like, "I really wasn't all that bad; I went to church regularly; I gave to the Red Cross almost every year and never cheated on my taxes." That boasting finished, then they would talk disparagingly about people of other races or cultures.

While we are quick to grab hold of the fact that we are forgiven and therefore redeemed (or bought back from the devil), our thought life is possibly still controlled by the evil one. If so, it's not surprising that we are sometimes guilty of transgressions from our previous life. That's why we must be alert to what we say and do--so we can instantly go before the throne with godly repentance.

We need to fully understand these truths and how they apply to us: "There is therefore now no condemnation to them which are in Christ Jesus, who walk not after the flesh [our former life], but after the Spirit [of God]. For the law of the Spirit of life in Christ Jesus hath made me free from the law of sin and death. For what the law could not do, in that it was weak through the flesh, God sending His own Son in the likeness of sinful flesh, and for sin, condemned sin in the flesh" (Romans 8:1-3).

It is imperative we know we have been set free from the law of sin and death. We don't have to do what they do or say what they say. We must say what God says or repent and seek forgiveness. That is one of the many doors to freedom, and forgiveness could be the key to whatever door seems locked against you.

A very soft-spoken woman came to the prayer room one evening, looking every bit of nine-months pregnant. She wanted us to pray that her husband would come back. He had left the week before, leaving her with eight children and this ninth child due any moment. Without knowing any more than the barest details, we asked that the Lord God forgive him and agreed, according to Matthew 18:19, that he would return home and ask their forgiveness for leaving.

Well, the next Friday, just before the main meeting, the woman ran up to me all aglow. I thought I knew what she was going to say-- but did I ever have a surprise.

"I want you to know the prayers really worked," she said. "Just as we agreed, my husband came home Tuesday and asked us to forgive him and asked if he could come back and live with us." I am always thrilled how God confirms prayers of agreement with almost shocking accuracy. But as I was watching her, a cloud seemed to engulf her face and she said, "But *they* keep telling me they are going to kill the baby."

"*Who* keeps telling you they're going to kill the baby?" I asked incredulously. "These voices." she said. When I had recovered from the shock, I said, "You'd better come to the prayer room after the meeting."

When I got there, she and a number of others were already waiting for me. As yet, I hadn't shared this with any of the others, because we hadn't been all that heavy into deliverance. In fact, though Toots and I had several experiences with deliverance, either directly or being in on other people's sessions, I'm not certain this wasn't a first in the prayer room.

After filling in the others on the joyous part, about her husband's return in answer to our prayers, I felt obligated to tell them about this new wrinkle on the face of our spiritual progress. Like me, they were astonished. So I sat the woman down and asked her a few key questions. At least, they seemed key questions to me at the time. But I ask you to keep in mind that all our experience in deliverance could be stuffed up a gnat's nostril. It wasn't until years later that I learned Jesus didn't ask a lot of dumb questions. He just went ahead and got the job done.

The first thing I asked was whether she had ever indulged in any occult practices--horoscopes, seances, fortune-telling, table-tilting, Ouija boards, anything that would allow Satan to get a foothold in her life.

"I'm a good Catholic," she said. "I wouldn't do any of that stuff." Then I asked--having recently learned what a serious thing unforgiveness is and how Satan can use it against the children of light-- whether she knew of any unforgiveness in her life. I pointed out that it could go back to her childhood--like someone doing something to her and causing her to swear to get even. Her answer was, "No, I am a very forgiving person. I don't hold anything against anybody."

Well, Lord, I wondered, *where do we go from here? I don't know what else to ask.* It was then the thought came to me that Jesus died for our forgiveness. So I began to softly pray while (for whatever reason) keeping my eyes on her--perhaps by the leading of the Holy Spirit, you imagine? Whatever, I prayed something like this:

Heavenly Father, we come before You in the Name of Jesus-- seeking how we can help this child. You not only know her need, Father, but what we here can do. She says she has no unforgiveness in her life, Father. So, as Jesus stood in the position of forgiveness for us, I stand in the position of forgiveness for anything she may have forgotten.

At this moment, as I was standing in forgiveness for her, she barked like a dog. It almost scared us out of our wits but we quickly recovered, knowing now what (if not yet who) we were dealing with.

I began to command it to come out--and to name itself. I said four or five times, "I command you, in the Name of Jesus, to come out of this woman. And I command you to name yourself." All the time I was doing this, the woman's nose was twitching and her mouth was going through every type of grimace. But finally the thing came out with a whine: "*Witchcraft,*" it said, and the woman slumped over and crumbled to the floor. If she hadn't been obviously breathing, you would have thought she was dead. But in just a few moments, her eyes began to flutter and she came awake with a start, asking, "What happened? Where have I been?"

Do you know what happened and where she had been? I know she was delivered of a demon whose name was Witchcraft--but as to where she had been, I don't know. I only know that the key to getting her back to us was forgiveness--a key that unlocks the doors to many afflictions. Search your hearts, people--it is very important for your release from many areas of bondage.

Some of the people in the prayer room asked if I thought the woman had lied about involvement in the occult. Any answer I might have given would have been pure speculation. But there is a scripture I have been meditating on for years--and I believe it is vastly more important than we know. In fact, millions of our young people may one day have to face the issue it addresses. When Samuel confronted King Saul with his disobedience to the word of the Lord, Samuel said, "Rebellion is as the sin of witchcraft, and stubbornness is as iniquity and idolatry" (1 Samuel 15:23).

So I will ask *you* a question: instead of lying, is it possible that the woman had been rebellious and stubborn all her life, thus allowing the spirit of witchcraft to come in? And where do *we* stand with iniquity and idolatry?

This would really be a good place to stop and search our hearts, wouldn't it? Or now how about asking the Lord to reveal that to us in a prayer? Perhaps like this:

Father, I know Your Word says that rebellion is as the sin of witchcraft and stubbornness is as iniquity and idolatry. Rebellion and stubbornness so often reveal the worst elements of self in me. So Father, in the Name of Jesus, I ask that the light of Your Holy Spirit shine into those dark recesses of my inner man to search out those places I have failed to detect. And if there is any rebellion, I ask that You help me turn it to obedience--and if there is any stubbornness, that You help me turn it to loving humility. I know I can best serve You when I am instantly obedient and

openly humble. All this, Father, I ask in the Name that is above
every name.   *Amen—and Amen*

5
Healing, Health and Wholeness Through Obedience and Action

Go . . . shew thyself to the priest
Read Matthew 8:1-4

"Go . . . shew thyself to the priest." Jesus prefaced this commandment with these instructions: "See thou tell no man." Although we
have gone over this scripture in a previous chapter, I want to show
you a different approach here. After laying His hands on the leper
and saying, "I will; be thou clean," Jesus tells us that immediately his
leprosy was cleansed. This miracle was performed before a great
multitude--so why didn't the Lord just let the miracle testify of itself
and go on about His business? Was there something more He
wanted accomplished? Yes, there was.

In the Old Testament, whenever there was a miracle to be performed, God or Moses or one of the prophets commanded a person
(or sometimes the people) to *do* something, which, when they were
obedient, brought forth some mighty work. It was the same with
Jesus, Peter, Paul and others in the New Testament when they ministered under the anointing of God. Here again we see that the Lord
God rarely did anything on His own, i.e., without working in and
through man.

When it is our desire to please God, it is thrilling to know He
says, "Let us . . . " Often we fail to see the aspect of God's nature that
says, "How about you and me doing some nifty things together?" But
instead of waiting for big Daddy-Papa to come on the scene--who
never hurries and is never late--we catch the vision and go skipping

across the meadow, only to stumble over a cow. Because of this kind of spiritual blindness, we tend to err in the most important of all areas: the reason the Lord gives us visions is so that we (i.e., He and you and I) can work out the details together, coming to a glorious finish together. Visions were never meant to be foot races to see who can get there the fastest. Even if we have to go at a snail's pace, what difference does it make as long as He is beside us?

There is such superlative wisdom in the Book of James, which exhorts us, "Count it all joy when ye fall into divers [or a variety of] temptations; knowing this, that the trying [or testing] of your faith worketh patience [even to the restraining of your inclination to run ahead of the Lord]. But let patience have her perfect work, that ye may be perfect and entire [or mature and, therefore, serene], wanting nothing [or having every need met]" (James 1:2-4).

In the chapter on faith we saw that faith in God is believing His promises and trusting Him to fulfill them. Also we saw that another aspect of faith is standing staunch in the face of adversity and stepping out in the confident assurance of His unfailing support. This is shown in James, which says, "Thou hast faith, and I have works: shew me thy faith *without* thy works, and I will shew thee my faith *by* my works" (James 2:18).

Although this would seem very similar to the obedience factor there is an important ingredient missing. In the matter of stepping out in faith, one is most often believing in his heart that what he is setting out to do will be accomplished and/or successful; obedience has to do with submission to command, compliance to demands or requests, i.e., doing what you're told.

This will be made clear as we go on. But first, I would like to set the stage with a few examples of obedience. When God told Noah to make an ark of gopher wood--450 feet long, 75 feet wide, and 45 feet high--Noah didn't say, "Lord God, You've gotta be kiddin'." Despite the fact he had never seen an ark--nor quite possibly rain, for that matter--Noah got his ax and his adz and went to work for 120 years. And Abram (whom God would rename Abraham), at age 58 and with a barren wife, took God at His word when God told him, "Get thee out of thy country, and from thy kindred, and from thy father's house, unto a land that I will shew thee: and I will make of thee a great nation" (Genesis 12:1,2). Instead of laughing hysterically and falling on the floor, Abram obeyed God, thereby entering into one of the most miraculous lives ever recorded.

Then we see God speaking to Moses over and over again from the backside of the desert of Midian to the shores of the Red Sea-- and from the Wilderness of Shur to Mount Nebo. And though we read of God most often referring to him as "My servant, Moses," we have seen also that God "spoke to him face to face, as a man speaketh unto his friend." And as Moses was obedient and took whatever action God commanded, he and the children of Israel experienced miracle after miracle, from Exodus through Deuteronomy. Moses was God's instrument in setting the plagues before Pharaoh; opening the Red Sea; casting the tree in the bitter waters to make them sweet; supplying meat and bread by having God send the quail and the manna; striking the rock to get crucially needed water. All of these miracles--and many more--resulted from Moses' acts of obedience (Exodus 3-13).

Also because of their obedience, Joshua, Gideon, Samson, Ruth, Samuel, David, Solomon, Esther, Job, Elijah, Elisha--and most of the Old Testament prophets--were able to see the hand of God.

When we get to the New Testament, however, although the obedience factor doesn't change, the power structure now comes by and through the man Jesus. As He gave us example after example and demonstration after demonstration--so we would know how obedience works--He gave the power (authority) to us. Now as we are obedient to His Word, we can see the promised signs and wonders follow.

Every Christian who wants to serve God in the beauty of holiness should make a study of obedience. When you do, you will discover some really nifty stuff. For in nearly every instance where God or Jesus told (or commanded) someone to do something to receive a miracle, that person had the right or privilege to say no with impunity. However, I must say I haven't run across too many people with the courage to disobey a clear mandate from the Lord. What most are guilty of is disobedience to His will rather than out-and-out disobedience to His spoken word.

But in either or both cases, like Jesus, we say, "Father, forgive them; for they know not what they do" (Luke 23:34)--to which I add, "nor what they're missing."

Stretch forth thy hand
Read Luke 6:6-11

After Jesus said to the man with the withered hand, "Rise up, and stand forth in the midst," the Word says the man arose and stood forth. That was his first act of obedience. Notice also that Jesus didn't say, "Would you kindly stand forth?" He said, "Rise up, and stand forth." It was a command, not an "if thou wilt."

This happened on a sabbath--mostly because Jesus was forever trying to *oosh* the Jews past their traditions to see things in the light of truth, rather than in what Satan was always showing them. But "the scribes and Pharisees watched Him, whether He would heal on the sabbath day; that they might find an accusation against Him." The Word then says, "He knew their thoughts, and said to the man which had the withered hand, Rise up." Then Jesus said, "I will ask you one thing; Is it lawful on the sabbath days to do good, or to do evil? to save life, or to destroy it? And looking round about upon them all, He said unto the man, Stretch forth thy hand. And he did so; and his hand was restored whole as the other." This was the second act of obedience.

Have you ever wondered what would have happened if the man had said (in the first instance), "I refuse to be made a laughing-stock"? Or if he had indeed stood forth, all right, but when the Lord told him (in the second instance) to stretch forth his hand, what would have happened if he had said, "The reason why it's hanging down here is it's withered"?

Again, what would have happened if, when Jesus told the blind man to go to the Pool of Siloam, he had said, "If I knew where the Pool of Siloam is, why would I need You?" And when the Lord Jesus told the leper to go and show himself to the priest, what if the leper had said, "Would You mind waiting till Tuesday? I have a very important appointment"?

Although we are pretty certain nothing of any consequence would have happened, we also know that none of these speculations is relevant--because all were obedient and all were healed.

In Matthew 9 and John 5, there are two other occasions where the obedience (or action) factor is an integral part of Jesus' healing ministry. We have dealt with the Matthew incident in an earlier chapter, viewing the incident in relation to grace and truth, but here we will be looking at the obedience aspect.

The man with the palsy was carried by four men who--when they couldn't get to Jesus for the multitude jamming the entrance to the house where He was--broke through the roof tiling and let the man down right in front of the Lord. If you have forgotten, the account says, "And Jesus seeing their faith said unto the sick of the palsy, Son, be of good cheer; thy sins be forgiven thee" (Matthew 9:2). The scribes were appalled and said within themselves, "This Man blasphemeth." The chief priests and elders considered blasphemy a stoning offense. The Lord knew their thoughts. And He asks which they think is easier, "to say, Thy sins be forgiven thee; or to say, Arise and walk?" Without so much as a peep from them, He turns to the sick man and commands, "Arise, take up thy bed, and go unto thine house" (Matthew 9:6). And the palsied man was instantly obedient, leaped up, took his bed and departed to his house.

Suppose he had said, "Lord, I'm still a little weak--and I know my four friends are waiting for me." Instead of carrying his bed, he would have died in it.

The man in John 5:2-9 was somewhat unique apparently, because the Bible calls him *a certain man*--not just *a man*, not just *a
lame or an impotent man*, but *a certain man*. Instead of being *a guy*
named John Smith, think how much nicer to be *a certain man* named
John Smith. Anyway, as we follow the story, there are some very interesting aspects I am still asking the Lord to reveal to me in depth
(for I have been meditating on this story for a very long time).

Since it is my intention to paraphrase, I would recommend you
slowly and carefully take in the whole story (John 5:1-16). Reading
and meditating on it--chewing on it as a cow does her cud, so to say--
will bring forth many peculiar (if delightful) truths of God.

Jesus went up to Jerusalem for a feast of the Jews and, as He
passed the Pool of Bethesda, which was right near the sheep market,
He saw *a certain man*. Around the pool lay a great multitude of impotent folk--blind, halt, withered--waiting for the moving of the
waters. For an angel came down from time to time and stirred up
the waters, and the first person to step down into the pool after the
stirring of the waters was always healed of his affliction.

What an air of expectancy must have surrounded that area! Although Jesus may or may not have had compassion on the multitude
--as is so often recorded in the Word--on this particular day He
seemed to have eyes only for this "certain man . . . which had an infirmity thirty and eight years." We have seen that Jesus had great discernment throughout the scriptures and so it was in this case. For
the Word says that He knew the man had been in that condition for
a long time (John 5:6). Then the Lord, singling out the man, stood
over him--for he was lying on a bed (Greek, *krabbatos*, meaning
"mattress")--and quietly asked, "Wilt thou be made whole?"

Notice I said "quietly"--and I am quite frankly indulging in
human logic here thinking that if Jesus had shouted over the probable hubbub, He would have been mobbed. After all, everyone was
there looking to be healed--yes?

Following Jesus' question, one would think the man would have
answered, "You bet your dusty sandals." Or "Is the Pope Catholic?"

Or said something similar in the expression of the day. But the man answered in the negative: "I have no man, when the water is troubled, to put me into the pool: but while I am coming, another steppeth down before me" (John 5:7). At which point Jesus tells him, "Rise, take up thy bed, and walk." Then, "immediately the man was made whole, and took up his bed, and walked" (John 5:9).

Next, almost as an afterthought, the Bible says, "And on the same day was the sabbath." Isn't that just too charming for words? There really is a lot going on here: for the man was healed--or made whole--despite his negative attitude and confession, while he had quite possibly forgotten it was the sabbath. You can almost feel him blink. "The Jews therefore said unto him that was cured, It is the sabbath day: it is not lawful for thee to carry thy bed" (John 5:10). But tradition or no tradition, lawful or not lawful, the man was obedient to the Word and *immediately* took action.

If you are wondering what makes this incident odd or unusual, it is important you view it in the light of how most of the others were healed or made whole as an extension of obedience or action. For most others were healed as they went or as they stretched forth or as they came. This man was made whole while still lying on his mattress --and after an almost totally negative confession. How do you account for that?

For you needing healing or relief from something you have not yet fully understood--if you have the slightest inkling that obedience could be required--you might seek the Lord from this perspective:

Holy Father, I know You are omniscient (all-seeing and all-knowing) and I also know You are omnipresent (everywhere in all the earth and heavens) so I am confident that You not only know my need but are here this moment to hear my prayers and supplications. Father, if there is an action I am to take--or an obedience factor I need to know--I ask that by Your Holy Spirit You guide and lead me to the answer. For Your Word says, When the Spirit of truth is come, He will guide and lead me into all

*truth. And, Lord God, You know my failings in the matter of
being sensitive to the things of Your Spirit--and I consider that a
part of Your truth--so I ask that I be taught of the Spirit those
things that will make me a living witness to Your limitless truth.
And whether by scripture--or by the word of one of Your servants
--I seek to know all the areas of obedience in which I can help
others as well as myself. Because I have asked, Father--and Your
Word assures I will have an answer--I thank You in Jesus' Name.*

Amen--and Amen

Go and wash in Jordan seven times
Read 2 Kings 5

Though the Lord Jesus gave us enough examples of the obedience
factor to fill a book, we are deviating here to an excellent Old Testament example of both disobedience (or rebellion) and obedience.
Also, along with these two truths, we see the result of bitterness and
covetousness.

Naaman was a great captain in the eyes of his master, the king
of Syria, because Naaman was a mighty man of valor--and he and
the host he commanded had delivered Syria from their oppressors.
But the Word says he was a leper.

Think of how dreadful that was--and how devastating to have
reached the very pinnacle of success only to find you have an incurable disease, that you are indeed leprous. And just because you
are at the top of the heap doesn't change the fact that you are considered unclean, even by your lowliest servant.

But Naaman was in for a world-shaking experience. The Lord
God of Israel had allowed him to capture a little (Jewish) maiden
who became the servant to Naaman's wife. It was this little maid-
servant who had the boldness to say to her mistress, "Would God my
lord (Naaman) were with the prophet that is in Samaria. For he
would recover him of his leprosy."

Have you ever considered what would have happened if Naaman and his family had been anti-Semitic? But they weren't and in

his desperation Naaman set out immediately for Samaria. And he brought a letter from his king to the king of Israel, saying, "Now when this letter is come unto thee, behold, I have therewith sent Naaman my servant to thee, that thou mayest recover him of his leprosy." Wow! Imagine all the thoughts that raced through the mind of the king of Israel.

The Word says, "And it came to pass, when the king of Israel had read the letter, that he rent [or tore] his clothes, and said, Am I God, to kill and make alive, that this man doth send unto me to recover a man of his leprosy? Wherefore consider, I pray you, and see how he seeketh a quarrel against me."

Here the Bible rolls out one of its big guns--Elisha, the man of God, the great prophet who is living under the anointing of a double portion of Elijah's God-given power. He hears about the king rending his clothes and sends to ask why. Though the Bible doesn't say the king informed him about Naaman, it does say Elisha told the king of Israel, "Let him [Naaman] come now to me, and he shall know that there is a prophet in Israel."

But when this great man, Naaman, comes to the prophet's house, Elisha doesn't even bother to go out to see him! Instead, he sends his servant with a message, saying, "Go and wash in the Jordan seven times, and thy flesh shall come again to thee, and thou shalt be clean." Could anything be simpler? All that was required was obedience.

Yet Naaman was furious--with a little prompting from the evil one, of course. You see, times haven't changed much and neither have people. Naaman had it all figured out how God ought to heal him, because he said, "Behold, I thought, he [the prophet] will surely come out to me [seeing who I am], and stand, and call on the Name of the Lord his God, and strike his hand over the place, and recover the leper."

To you who are afflicted: have you told the Lord God how He should heal you? Have you given it a lot of thought and come up with the ideal solution, as Naaman had? If you have, then I have this bit of news for you--better you should figure out how you're going to die. You will most likely be a lot closer to right.

God is not all that impressed with how you think it should be done any more than He was impressed with Naaman's thoughts. Just to refresh your memory, He says, "I am the Lord, I change not" (Malachi 3:6), nor is He likely to turn to you for advice. So, beloved, if you are seeking relief from some sort of affliction, you had best seek *His* way, which, I assure you, is the best.

You can see that Naaman continues with his reasoning, saying, "Are not Abana and Pharpar, rivers of Damascus, better than all the waters of Israel? May I not wash in them, and be clean? So he turned and went away in a rage [which was quite possibly inspired by demonic activity]." It is easy to see that, if it hadn't been for his servants and their humble wisdom, Naaman would have been forced to go home to die. But one of the servants said, "My father, if the prophet had bid thee do some great thing, wouldest thou not have done it? How much rather then, when he saith to thee, Wash, and be clean?"

Now here comes the good stuff--the non-fattening mashed potatoes and gravy. One verse says it all: "Then went he [Naaman] down, and dipped himself seven times in Jordan, according to the saying of the man of God: and his flesh came again like unto the flesh of a little child, and he was clean." Obedience and action--a simple but effective little combo, eh? Do any of you think that, if Naaman hadn't dipped himself in Jordan seven times, he would have been healed--ever? What if he had only dipped six times? Well, I know you get the picture.

Stand upright on thy feet
Read Acts 14:8-10

Here we see another *certain man* at Lystra, who was "impotent in his feet, being a cripple from his mother's womb, who never had walked: the same heard Paul speak: who steadfastly beholding him, and perceiving he had faith to be healed, said with a loud voice, Stand upright on thy feet. And he leaped and walked." When this impotent man made the first gesture toward obedience, God made it possible for him to leap and walk.

Over the years, the Lord has shown us many miracles following obedience and action. Also, sad to say, we have seen all too many who refused to take that first step and thereby failed to receive what God was offering them. But we won't dwell on the negatives; we are just going to rejoice over those who went past their natural man, thereby winding up in the supernatural realm of the miraculous.

In chapter two, we told about the young girl who had just been told she was paralyzed from the waist down and quite possibly would never be able to walk again. But God didn't see it that way. For when I asked her if she would like to walk and if she was willing to walk, and she said yes, I acted like Peter at the Beautiful Gate. I took her by the right hand and said, "In the Name of Jesus Christ of Nazareth, rise up and walk," and like the man at Lystra, she leaped and walked. Obedience and action.

Then there was the night at a Franciscan church in New York. A Franciscan priest ministered the Word of God, after which I ministered to the sick. Although there were numbers of dynamic healings, by far the most astonishing was the healing of a Bishop Joseph.

He was nearly the last in line. It seemed to us that he had held back, waiting to see if all this stuff was really of the Lord. But when he came to whatever conclusion, two strong men--one on each side--carried him forward with his feet barely touching the floor. Apparently he was able to stand--if ever so uncertainly--but the two men stood close behind him ready to catch him should one of his attacks come on. He had a severe heart condition and, according to his testimony, his doctors had told him he could go at any moment. But he had one great thing going for him: he had no fear of dying.

As I agreed with him in prayer and laid hands on him, commanding his heart to get in line with God's Word, the Lord said in that wonderful quiet way of His, "Tell him to run around the room." Man! *Lord!* I thought but didn't say, *that's a hard saying.* But to

Bishop Joseph, I said, "The Lord would have you run around the room."

Irish astonishment ran around his face. And if his eyebrows had shot any higher, they would have knocked his zucchetto (that little red skull cap) off. "Me biy," he said in his great brogue, "you wouldn't be puttin' me on, would ye?" I looked him straight in his owlish eyes and repeated, "Run around the room." As he turned away from me very slowly, he kept looking at me over his shoulder, waiting to see if I was going to back down, I guess. But the Lord and I stood firm--or, at least, He stood firm. All I could say was, *"Goodness, Lord--mercy, Lord."*

When I didn't budge, Bishop Joseph began to shuffle along, taking two-to-three-inch steps. After a few feet, his steps were eight-to-ten inches and then half a normal step--until he got ten-to-fifteen feet away--and then a full step, leading into a shuffling trot. Although he never got to a full gallop, everyone began applauding--and it was a true miracle of God. He ran around that whole, big room (maybe 75' x 100'). And when he got back to me--face shining like an Irish angel--he said with great glee, "And I'm not even breathin' hard!" Obedience and action.

On yet another occasion in the prayer room at Georgetown, I again had one of those breathtaking experiences. This woman was all but carried in by two men. When I asked what was wrong, she said that she had an affliction which caused all the bones in her feet to be out of joint. Just to put her foot on the floor under her full weight was an agonizing experience. So I asked if she would like to be healed by the Lord Jesus--to which she said yes. "Can you believe, when I lay hands on you, that the Lord will heal you?" was my next question. When she answered yes this time, I told her about the prayer of agreement in Matthew 18 and quoted that part of Mark 16 where Jesus said, "These signs shall follow them that believe . . . they shall lay hands on the sick, and they shall recover" (Mark 16:17,18).

Then, just as I was concluding my brief prayer, the Lord said, "Have her stamp her feet." I was shocked. I said (within myself),

*Lord that is outrageous! These people already think I'm some kind of
kook.* But to her--in obedience and action--I said, "The Lord wants
you to stamp your feet." I knew I had to stand there and look un-
shakably confident but I assure you that wasn't what I felt. As for
her, she looked at me as though I hadn't heard anything she said and
let me know, "That would be excruciating."

Though I shuddered inwardly, I asked, "Do you believe a loving
God would hurt one of His children?" When she shook her head no
somewhat tentatively, I said, "Then you will have to trust Him."

I gave her my hand and she stood up, very gingerly, and stood
there a long while. You could see the battle going on--her face regis-
tering every emotion--until we could see she had made her decision.
She raised one foot and put it down firmly, looking completely
surprised. Then she took her first firm step, then another and
another--until she was walking around the room, stamping her feet
and jumping up and down.

Obedience and action--plus the miraculous intervention of a
merciful God--not only healed the woman's feet but lifted an enormous burden off me.

All three of these people had a choice--to be obedient or not to
be obedient. The young girl could have said, "But the doctor said--"
and Bishop Joseph could have said, "If I can't walk, how am I going
to run?" and the woman with the disjointed feet could have said, "I've
never heard of anything so outrageous. Couldn't God do it some
other way?" But all were obedient--and all were healed.

If I may but touch His clothes
Read Mark 5:25-34; Luke 8:43-48

"If I may but touch His clothes. . . . " This was said by the woman
with the issue of blood in Mark 5 and Luke 8. Though we have dis-
cussed this incident in an earlier chapter, here we are going to look
at it from the *obedience* and *action* points of view.

The scriptures tell us the woman had this affliction for twelve years, that she had spent all of her money on doctors--"and was nothing bettered, but rather grew worse."

Then it says of her, "When she had heard of Jesus, [she] came in the press behind, and touched His garment. For she said, If I may touch but His clothes, I shall be whole" (Mark 5:27,28).

Earlier, as we looked at the Naaman story, we saw that he had already figured out how God was supposed to heal him--his way, not God's way. He would have possibly had faith for *his* way but he disdained God's way and was furious. And if it hadn't been for one of his servants convincing him to try God, he would have gone back to Damascus in a rage, to die a grim and ugly death.

The parallel here is that both came for healing, the difference being that Naaman traveled well over a hundred miles, while we don't know that the woman didn't live on the very street where Jesus was traveling. But that isn't the point. Both heard, both made the decision and both came--regardless of the difficulties or inconvenience. Yet neither of them would have been healed if they hadn't been obedient and taken the necessary action. Naaman had to go and wash in Jordan seven times: he had to be willing (or obedient) and he had to go and wash. In the case of the woman, despite how debilitated she was, or how miserable she felt, she had to make her way through the crowd to touch Jesus' clothes.

The revelation here is that God, who is forever trying to reach us with His lovingkindness, saw that Naaman received His message of love through a little captive Jewish servant and that the woman received her message by way of an open heart. I wonder what would have happened if Naaman had said, "Samaria is over a hundred miles. I wonder if the prophet could come to me. After all, if God really loved me . . . " Or if the woman had said, "I wish He could have come Friday when I felt a lot stronger. But if God really loves me, He can send Jesus back this way."

Vanity can have absolutely no place in the healing process--and pride is the biggest of all the no-nos. In the little book of Ec-

clesiastes, Solomon writes of vanity some thirty times, pointing out
its traps and snares, calling it an "an evil disease" (Ecclesiastes 6:2).
And the Word has not one good thing to say about pride. Solomon
says in Proverbs, "The fear [reverence] of the Lord is to hate evil:
pride, and arrogancy, and the evil way, and the froward mouth, do I
hate" (Proverbs 8:13). It is easily seen here that when God lists
Pride's cohorts, He puts Pride as their leader, the captain under Evil.
Also Solomon says, "A man's pride shall bring him low: but honor
shall uphold the humble in spirit" (Proverbs 29:23).

Why am I suddenly introducing pride and vanity into the picture? Because they are among the greatest hindrances to obedience
and action. Almost from the day we are born we are taught to be
proud of our color, our looks, our neighborhood, our accomplish-
ments, our church, our religion . . . our . . . our . . . my . . . my . . .
Then as we accept the fact that we are somehow better than "they"
are, pride tells us to stick out our chest and vanity tells us to have it
custom-fitted. This, of course, is the evidence: I am me; I can do it
better; I am superior.

On that day when Reckoning comes in and occupies our easy
chair by the fireplace with his briefcase full of sickness and
affliction--and all attempts to do it ourselves fail to budge him--then
we begin to wonder in our hearts, *What happened?* Quite suddenly
the evil one reminds us of God and we ask, "God, where are You
when I need You?" A deathly silence follows--Amen? But He hasn't
gone anywhere: He has always been there in Everywheresville. But
we haven't been able to focus on Him for focusing on us.

In this area, beloved, we must see the truth. That deceiving
spirit that has led us around by the nose--our coach and mentor in
the ways of evil, pride, vanity, arrogance and a bragging mouth--
doesn't just get up and leave. Nor does he melt. He stays around to
help us with such thoughts as *If God really loved me, He* . . .

Pride and vanity are two of the three things for which Satan was
thrown out of heaven, the third being iniquity. The Bible says of him,
"Thou wast perfect in thy ways from the day that thou wast created,

till iniquity was found in thee. . . . Thine heart was lifted up [with vanity] because of thy beauty, thou hast corrupted thy wisdom by reason of thy brightness [or pride of accomplishment]" (Ezekiel 28:15,17). You see, Lucifer (who became Satan) was a created being, designed to be perfect. But when vanity, pride and arrogance caused him to covet the throne of God (see Isaiah 14; Ezekiel 28), God regarded those evils as iniquity. And when He saw that Lucifer had been irrevocably deceived by the thoughts and intents of his own heart, it was necessary that he (Lucifer/Satan) be deposed. God was not about to allow a created being to usurp the authority of his Creator. That would be like the clay comparing itself to the potter.

The thought that we are able to somehow be deceived is one of those hard sayings that is especially difficult to hear. What we fail to comprehend is that the deceiver (the dragon, that old serpent, called the Devil and Satan, who deceives the whole world) is not in the least intimidated by what we say or think as long as we don't say or think he exists. When we do, all of his cunning lies and fraudulent deception can be put before the light and exposed. But when we are convinced we are too smart for him, he uses all of our self-deception--and packages it under a new label, sometimes Pride and sometimes Vanity.

To guard against the wiles of the devil, we must first *know the Truth* (Jesus is the Truth), who will make us free (see John 8:32). So, if you have any doubts about where you stand with either pride or vanity--and whether indeed they are a cause of hindrance in matters of obedience and action--you might wish to pray this prayer:

Lord God, possessor of heaven and earth, I come before You this day in the Name of Jesus Christ of Nazareth, holding up to Your light all my rights and privileges. I want to know they are not tainted by any fleshly or carnal state of being. Almighty God, I do want to have a healthy respect for myself and what You are making of me but I also wish to be certain that I never offend You through any inordinate self-esteem, conceit, pride, insolence or ar-

rogance. It is my desire to be sensitive to Your every wish, that in my instant obedience and positive actions I will be able to flow freely in Your channel of blessings, glorying in the wonders of my God and the Lord Jesus Christ.   *Amen--and Amen*

6
Healing, Health and Wholeness Through Speaking the Word

Wilt thou be made whole?
Read John 5:1-16

"Wilt thou be made whole?" What a question! Can you imagine any answer that wasn't in the affirmative? But that is what the Son of God asked. Do you feel He had any doubt as to whether that man wanted to be made whole? Since the Lord had received the Spirit without measure--an unlimited amount of God's Spirit--would He lack such simple discernment? Doesn't pretty much everyone wish to be whole? Of course they do and of course Jesus knew it absolutely.

But let me lay a few "what ifs" on you. What if a person enjoyed the sympathy and attention he might not receive if he were healthy and whole? Would the Lord just go ahead and heal him anyway? And what if a person doubted the Word of God and didn't believe He still heals, that healing went out with the apostles? Would the God of all love overrule his unbelief? What if rebellion or vanity or pride ruled the thoughts of a person so he felt he should be healed just because of who or what he was. Would the Lord of glory just go ahead and do His thing?

All scripture except John 5 would indicate otherwise. Here we see the Lord Jesus seeming to violate every doctrine He had previously set forth. Is that possible? Although He is the Son of God--God Himself, if you will--does He have the right to introduce confusion into His Word to man? What think ye?

Well, one of the most glorious things God has taught me is that
I must leave Him room to be God. I cannot continue to look on the
outward appearance--to be swayed by what I have heard, what I have
seen, thought or felt. God has definitely not made me His judge.
And since He has given me every right and privilege to be what and
who I desire--to exercise my will in any way I choose--can I possibly
allow Him any less? Of course not.

As we look at John 5:1-16, the seeming contradiction must not
be viewed in the negative. We must see it as God being God, working through the Son of man to reveal that He quite possibly knows
more than we.

Many of us, not knowing what Jesus knew, would have left the
man lying there in his affliction. After some of the faith teaching by
those who grab hold of bits and pieces of the truth, we could be
guilty of looking at the man in the light of his being in that condition
for thirty-eight years. Being convinced that he didn't have the faith to
be healed, we would dismiss him and go about our more worthwhile
pursuits. But that would be error--that would be making the impera-
tives of God ineffectual.

In the chapter on obedience and action, we read that this man
was made whole before he showed any obedience or action, which is
contrary to all other like incidents. Did the Lord make a mistake?
Was He impatient to get to the temple? I don't believe so; there is
no indication Jesus was ever in a hurry. He was unalterably perfect
and the only apparent impatience He ever showed could be counted
as conjecture on our parts. For we don't really know, when He said,
"How long shall I be with you? How long shall I suffer you?" (Mark
9:19) that He didn't say it with the tired smile you might use with
children. After all, He often addressed His disciples as "little
children."

Everything else about this incident in John 5 notwithstanding, it
is vital that we see that Jesus' words, "Rise, take up thy bed, and
walk," were *with power*. They lifted the man to his feet, gave him
strength to bend over and take up his mattress and walk.

When you have a need--and what you say must be used as a
force--are your words endowed with power from on high? That is
what we will be dealing with in this chapter. If you are a born-again,
Spirit-filled believer, your words can heal the sick, cleanse the lepers,
raise the dead and cast out devils (or demons)--because you have
been freely given the power (Matthew 10:8). However, if you don't
believe this--if Satan has convinced you that you are somehow
inadequate--your words can be just words, little puffs of wind, hollow
sounds that will never shake anything.

He rebuked the fever
Read Matthew 8:14,15 ; Mark 1:29-34; Luke 4:38-41
When Peter's mother-in-law was sick with a fever, the Word says
that Jesus rebuked the fever (Luke 4:39). While Matthew 8:14,15
and Mark 1:29-31 don't have the Lord rebuking the fever--but have
Him touching her hand and taking her by the hand and lifting her
up--we see enough incidences where He spoke the word to demons,
afflictions and even a fig tree to know that these were examples for
us to follow.

The Luke scripture is particularly interesting because there are
no side complexities to divert us. Jesus arose from His seat in the
synagogue and entered into Simon Peter's house. "And Simon's
wife's mother was taken with a great fever; and they besought Him
for her. And He stood over her, and rebuked the fever; and it left
her: and immediately she arose and ministered unto them" (Luke
4:38,39). Isn't that just fabulous?

Notice that Jesus didn't say anything to the mother-in-law but
spoke directly to the fever. It doesn't say whether or not this repre-
sented a mountain to Peter's wife's mother, but it does say it was a
great fever. So when we look at this incident in light of Mark's
gospel, which says, "Whosoever shall say unto this mountain, Be thou
removed, and be thou cast into the sea; and shall not doubt in his
heart, but shall believe that those things which he saith shall come to
pass; he shall have whatsoever he saith" (Mark 11:23), we see that

not only did Jesus get what He said but so did Peter's mother-in-law. Can you see that?

Few of us consider the power of our words--either for evil or for good. But the centurion at Capernaum truly understood the principle (see Matthew 8:5-10; Luke 7:1-10). For when Jesus volunteered to come and heal the centurion's palsied servant, he said, "I am not worthy that Thou shouldest come under my roof: But speak the Word only, and my servant shall be healed." The centurion then goes on to explain how he came to the knowledge of the importance of the spoken word: through his commands.

Oh, how frustrated the devil is going to be when the believers grab hold of this truth and begin putting it into practice! He and all his demons are going to run out of thumbs, trying to plug the holes in his dike.

You see, beloved, the Word says we get what we say. So if we are saying negative things--calling those things which seem to be what you think they really are instead of doing as God says, calling those things that be not as though they are--then the chances are you will be receiving a lot of vain imaginations in your life--whatever you are willing to speak.

For instance, have you ever said things like the following? "Boy--this is going to be another one of those days," or "Just as sure as we go to the beach with the kids, we're going to have a week of rain," or "Every year at this time, my sinuses start acting up, especially when it's damp." Of course, when you have planted that kind of poison-producing seed, you are not going to expect a crop of sweet corn or roses, eh? Because the Word of God says your crop will follow what you plant. In this instance, you will have bunches of lousy days, rain for your beach vacations, and sinus problems every year. Even worse, you can confess, "That's just my luck." Whew--doesn't that just make your skin crawl?

Out of the abundance of the heart
Read Matthew 12:34; Luke 6:45

"Out of the abundance of the heart the mouth speaketh." What a statement--and how important to us as believers. Addressing the Pharisees, Jesus said, "O generation of vipers, how can ye, being evil, speak good things? for out of the abundance of the heart the mouth speaketh" (Matthew 12:34). Then He goes on to say that a good man, out of the good treasure of his heart brings forth good things-- and an evil man evil things--winding up the complete thought with: "For by thy words thou shalt be justified, and by thy words thou shalt be condemned" Matthew 12:37).

So, beloved, I suppose the question here becomes, "How is your heart? Is it full of good treasures--open for all to see--or is it still in the murky deep, gathering seaweed, coral and barnacles?" In my own case, my testimony is that I am a good man with a good treasure because I have a good heart. That is not vanity, as it could well seem: I am merely conforming to what God says about me. Dare I do otherwise? How about you? Are you conforming to His Word concerning you, being the righteousness of God in Christ? For when you get this truth deep inside, you will be the matching pearl of great price (see Matthew 13:46).

There is almost no adequate way to express how important or far-reaching are the thoughts and intents of our hearts (or human spirits) and the words that flow out of them. Jesus said that by our words we are justified (the Greek word being *dikaioo*, meaning "made free or righteous") or by our words we are condemned (in the Greek, *katadikazo*, meaning "held in bondage or condemned to suffer imprisonment"). Can you see how seriously we must take what we say?

Over the years, as I learned to listen and hear what people said, I began to be aware of the patterns of sickness and affliction they bound to themselves through their words. They would say, "*my* arthritis, *my* cold, *my* ulcers, *my* stomach problem--*my* this and *my* that." Have you ever heard the expression, "You are possessed by your possessions"? Then think of what you are likely to have as you use *my* when describing sicknesses and afflictions. When you say "*my* whatever," that person or thing is bound to you and becomes your responsibility--"*my* car, *my* house, *my* electric bill, *my* wife, *my* children, *my* mother-in-law."

So I ask again, beloved, "How is your heart? And how is your confession? Are you saying what the Lord says about you, thus agreeing with His Word and entering into His channel of blessing? Or are you saying what you think and confessing how you feel?" Solomon warns us, "Thou art snared [trapped] with the words of thy mouth, thou art taken [captive] by the words of thy mouth" (Proverbs 6:2) . Instead of saying what we think, feel, have or have not, God wants us to confess (that we already have) our heart's desire, the abundance He promised, that all our needs are met and the health and wholeness He has assured us is ours right now. God is looking for us to do as He does: He desires us to call those things that be not as though they were (see Romans 4:17) despite the fact that in the physical or natural it may not seem so.

But, you might ask, if I confess I have something I don't really have, wouldn't I be telling a lie? The answer is no, of course, unless you would consider God a liar. Because God changed Abram's name to Abraham, saying, "For a father of many nations have I made thee [past tense]" (Genesis 17:5). God told him this when he was ninety-nine years old, thirteen years after Ishmael was born. And in an even more notable scripture, Jesus said, "God so loved [past tense] the world, that He gave [past tense] His only begotten Son, that whosoever believeth in Him should not perish, but have everlasting life" (John 3:16). Here Jesus is telling Nicodemus about Himself in the past tense--perhaps two and a half years before His death, burial and resurrection. Was Jesus a liar? Of course not. Throughout the Bible the Lord God speaks of the future in the present tense, as though it has already been accomplished.

One of the great examples of this future in the present is in Paul's epistle to the Ephesians, where he writes, "[God] hath raised us up together [past tense], and made us sit together [past tense] in heavenly places in Christ Jesus" (Ephesians 2:6). If you are seated in heavenly places in Christ Jesus, how can you be seated in the kitchen toasting a bagel?

Where do we learn to live in the future while actively pursuing the now? And how do we call into being those things that don't yet exist? One of the keys is revealed in Mark 11:24. After telling us about speaking to the mountain, Jesus goes on to say, "Therefore I say unto you, What things soever ye desire, when ye pray, believe that ye receive them, and ye shall have them."

On the surface, this would seem difficult, if not impossible, but it can't be either of those or Jesus wouldn't have recommended it so casually as a part of saying, praying and forgiving (Mark 11:22-26). You see, beloved, these things were part of His truth--and therefore as natural as breathing in and breathing out. Jesus was/is truth.

In our case, we need to swap our thinking from human logic and reasoning and see these truths from the divine perspective. In the natural, if we have the sales slip or the title deed to something and can walk on it, sit in it, play with it or climb it, it is unequivocally ours. But from the divine perspective, it already belongs to us long before the sales slip or the title deed ever arrive. Because the Lord says, in my favorite scripture, "Before they call [even from the foundation of the world], I will answer; and while they are yet speaking [or praying], I will hear" (Isaiah 65:24). That is like saying, "When we pray, believing, it is as though we put a substantial deposit on something that is to be meticulously custom-made. And since there is no lack of integrity (on either part), when it arrives, it will be perfect--and, of course, postpaid."

If you can't quite see this from God's perspective, you might approach Him with a relevant prayer:

Heavenly Father, You are forever showing us open secrets: yet those secrets are hard to grasp in the natural. So Father, I ask You in Jesus' Name to reveal how I am to believe for something I

*haven't yet received. There is no doubt here, my God, just the
desire to wholly understand how to fully enter in to its truth. For,
as the Bible assures me, Your Word is truth. So right now, Father,
it is the desire of my heart that* _____
_____ *[you fill in the
words]. And I further ask for that inner witness that will comfort
my heart and lead me in the path of complete understanding.*

Amen--and Amen

It shall be well
Read 2 Kings 4:8-37

"It shall be well." If your only son had just died in your arms, could
you make such a confession? Perhaps if you had an inordinate
amount of spiritual discernment you might, but most of us would
have experienced such overwhelming human emotions we would
have cried out, "Why my only son, God?" as though He was somehow responsible. But that isn't what the Shunamite woman did.

Every born-again, Spirit-filled believer should study and meditate on this story and the unique qualities of the Shunamite woman.
For whether by godly wisdom or human intuition, she really knew
how to use the words of her mouth. First off, we are told she was a
great woman. Then we see that she is also charitable and perceptive,
because she invited Elisha (the prophet) to eat bread before she perceived him to be a holy man of God. Had it been the other way
around--perceiving him to be a holy man and then inviting him to eat
bread--we would find her motives to be suspect. We might consider
that she wanted something out of him. But that wasn't the way it
was.

After perceiving him to be a holy man of God, she consults her
husband as to whether they might build him (Elisha) a little chamber
(or room) on the city wall with a bed, a table, a stool and a candle-
stick--so that "when he cometh . . . he shall turn in thither." Thus we
see she is not only spiritually perceptive but maritally astute as well--
understanding the need to consult her husband and, thereby, to be

pleasing to him. She didn't just go and do her thing and try to explain to her husband when the bills came in.

Another thing: when Elisha sees what she has done for him, he wants to know that her motives are right as well and has his servant, Gehazi, ask her what he (Elisha) can do for her. Does she desire him to speak to the king or to the captain of the host for her? Her answer was so beautiful, for she says very simply, "I dwell among mine own people." This shows us she was self-assured and confident --not having any social ambitions. She had no need of being elevated: she was strong and able to keep her own counsel.

Elisha then asks Gehazi (not the woman), "What then is to be done for her? And Gehazi answered [though the Bible doesn't say how he found out], Verily she hath no child, and her husband is old." It doesn't say that Elisha prayed or sought the Lord, he just tells Gehazi to call her. And when she stood in the door of Elisha's room, he said, "About this season, according to the time of life, thou shalt embrace a son."

Unlike Abraham and Sarah, who both fell into fits of hysterical laughter at the promise of a child when they were old, this great Shunamite woman was aghast, saying, "Nay, my lord, thou man of God, do not lie unto thine handmaid." This is one of the two times in the whole story where she seems to lose her composure. But the prophecy came to pass: "And the woman conceived, and bare a son at that season that Elisha had said unto her, according to the time of life." Was it perhaps here that the woman perceived that the *word* works?

I just love the Bible's brevity. For after she had conceived and borne a son, the very next verse begins with, "And when the child was grown, it fell on a day, that he went out to his father to the reapers." This account is like the account about Moses: he was taken out of the bulrushes by the daughter of Pharaoh and a few sentences later he is forty years old (see Exodus 2).

But here when it says the child was grown, I believe it simply means he was old enough to go to the fields alone. For when he says

to his father, while perhaps suffering a sunstroke, "My head, my head
. . . he [the father] said to a lad, Carry him to his mother. And when
he had taken him, and brought him to his mother, he sat on her
knees till noon, and then died."

After placing the dead child on the prophet's bed, she sends a
message to her husband, asking for an ass so she can go to the man
of God. When he inquires why she should go to Elisha, it neither
being new moon, nor sabbath, she quite simply says, "It shall be
well."

She then rides as fast as the ass can carry her the twenty miles
from Shunem to the prophet (Elisha) on Mount Carmel. And while
she is still at a distance, Elisha sees her and sends Gehazi to meet
her and ask her, "Is it well with thee? Is it well with thy husband? Is
it well with the child?" And she tells Gehazi, "It is well." How can she
say a thing like that? With the child already dead for at least five
hours! How could it possibly be well? Could it be that she refused to
accept defeat until she ran out of possibilities, until every hope had
been crushed?

The story winds up with her telling of the child's death; Elisha
sending Gehazi ahead with his staff to lay on the dead boy; with the
servant coming back to them en route to say there was no response;
with the final arrival of Elisha and the mother; at which point Elisha
"stretched himself upon the child; and the flesh of the child waxed
warm. Then he returned, and walked in the house to and fro; and
went up, and stretched himself upon him: and the child sneezed
seven times, and the child opened his eyes."

Elisha then presents the child to his mother; she falls at his feet
and takes up the child and leaves without further comment.

The whole thrust of this story is centered around the woman
saying, "It is well," every negative thing notwithstanding. In the face
of the most grim adversity--an appalling shock--she was able to say,
"It is well."

Can you say, "It is well" despite what you feel, think, see or
hear? If you are wondering, *Why should I?* I can tell you from ex-

perience that the good confession is the platform from which many miracles are launched.

Say to the mountain
Read Mark 11:23

Yes, we must learn to speak to it--whether a mountain of fear, oppression, debt, sickness or pain. Pain was my first big confrontation.

Toots and I were in Palm Beach. And one day as I was walking along the beach I saw a pallet (one of those wooden platforms forklift trucks use to lift things on and off loading docks) at the edge of the water. It had hundreds of tiny clams all over it and their necks were stretched forth, drowning. Clams drown in the air much the same as we would drown in the water. So I quickly pulled the pallet back into the water and launched it with a prayer, asking the heavenly Father to take care of the little ones, that they live and not die.

I pushed the pallet out into the waves and turned the outcome over to the living God, the Almighty One, the Possessor of heaven and earth, El Shaddai, the God of all glory and majesty. But the next wave pushed the pallet back toward shore. So Father's little helper-- definitely not thinking, for sure, not considering that God takes care of the whole earth day in and day out--was forced to get God out of a bind. Again, I pushed the pallet out to sea and again a wave pushed it back to shore. Yet again I pushed and yet again it came back. Now you know God can take care of a pallet and a few hundred clams and so do I. I just wasn't thinking.

This pallet had been in the ocean for a long time, so it was heavy and water-logged. Not only was it difficult to push, the fourth time, it came back across the top of my two feet--lightly, as a sort of warning. But I didn't get the message. The fifth time I pushed it out, a wave pushed it back across the top of my feet and lifted off my two big toenails. . . . The pain was not only electrifying, it was excruciating. I nearly fainted from shock.

As I saw the toenails dangling by shreds of flesh and the blood oozing out, I came to myself and shouted: "Pain, I speak to you in the Name of Jesus! I rebuke you and command you to leave!" Though my toes were still bleeding profusely, by the time I had walked up on the quay, the pain had left. Toots then rebuked the flow of blood and by the time the first-aid people and the lifeguard had come along, the bleeding had stopped.

But an all important principle was brought to light. From the first-aid people and the lifeguard, to the hospital attendants and doctors, every one of them (unwittingly, of course) tried to put pain back on me. Each one said the equivalent of, "Boy--that sure must be painful!" But each time, with the words of my mouth, I kept calling to nought (Psalm 33:10) their stout words. Three days later, I boarded the plane for Washington in a pair of brand-new brown suede shoes, because I had also rebuked any possible swelling.

Over the years, I rebuked warts, moles and many other forms of blemishes, commanding them to dry up from the root, according to the Word of God, and saw nothing but positive results. Then when a skin cancer the size of a small egg appeared behind and under my right arm, I knew it had to leave also. The Bible doesn't say, "The Word works--except in cases of cancer." The affliction began with an itching, stinging sensation, which, other than scratching it, I basically ignored--until one day when the cancer really started to bother me. When I raised my arm and looked in the mirror, I was quite surprised. My skin was a bright, fiery red and burned as though someone was holding a match to it.

"You foul and ugly thing, I speak to you in the Name of Jesus-- and I rebuke you--and command you to dry up from the root." I did this while looking at the cancer as though I was looking at an enemy, which, of course, it was. Also I rebuked the pain, and it left almost immediately. In a matter of days, the fiery redness began to diminish and in three months all that remained was little more than a small pinkish blotch the size of a dime.

Although I am not an authority on skin cancer--nor any other kind of cancer for that matter--the three or four I have seen were dead ringers for this one.

Right at the moment I am working on a big number--which I intend to annihilate before this book is finished. When it is gone, I will have a good report, with all the details.

To conclude this segment, I want you to know this: *There is a time to pray, and there is a time to say.* Ask the Lord which to do when.

7
Healing, Health and Wholeness
By God's Love and Jesus' Compassion

I have compassion on the multitude
Read John 8:1-11

"I have compassion. . . . " Jesus said this concerning the feeding of
the four thousand. And in numerous other places, the Word tells us
He either had compassion or told parables using compassion as the
central theme (Matthew 14:14; 18:27; Mark 1:41; 6:34; Luke 7:13;
10:33). However, the words for compassion differ in some places.
One word (in the Greek) is *splagchnizomai*, which means "to be
moved with compassion" or to have "bowels of yearning"--while the
word *eleeo* means "to have compassion, mercy or pity."

Regardless of which of the two words He used and how, the
resulting miracles or parables were phenomenal. It was with compassion that He fed the four thousand, healed a multitude of sick
people, cast the deaf and dumb spirit out of the epileptic boy, raised
the son of the widow of Nain from the dead and set the Gadarene
demoniac free from a legion of demons.

Love (in many of its forms) and charity are closely allied to
Jesus' compassion. This chapter will discuss compassion, love and
charity as they pertain to healing, health and wholeness. But first we
must see that what strife, resentment, bitterness and unforgiveness
are to illness and afflictions--love/compassion, charity, joy and peace
are to health and wholeness. There is no way to have love and compassion without total forgiveness, no matter who did what to whom.

One of the greatest examples of God's love is shown in John 8:1-11, where Jesus is in the temple teaching, when the scribes and Pharisees burst in upon Him. With them they had brought a woman taken in adultery. How is it possible for a woman to commit adultery without a man involved? Where was the man? Was he somehow absolved from any blame or guilt? Obviously there were two consenting adults, else it would have been rape--yes?

The Word doesn't say what the Lord thought or felt. But when these men accused the woman before Him, telling Him, "Moses in the law commanded us that such should be stoned; but what sayest Thou?" Jesus didn't answer them nor did He make any explanation to the multitude there in the temple. He just stooped and wrote on the ground, as though He hadn't heard them. When they persisted, He stood and said, "He that is without sin among you, let him first cast a stone at her." Could any answer be more gracious? It gave them permission to stone the woman, while being assured they couldn't stand before God without guilt if they did it. Isn't that remarkable wisdom?

Also we have to picture the woman. Since she was caught in the very act, as announced by the scribes and Pharisees, she was quite possibly disheveled and certainly terribly embarrassed and ashamed.

The Lord knew that stoning was not the answer; that kind of death would merely absolve her from her feelings of guilt, while doing absolutely nothing to keep her soul from hell. So, as these men were being convicted by their own conscience, Jesus again stooped and wrote on the ground until they had all left, "beginning at the eldest, even unto the last." Then when He again stood, seeing that He and the woman were there--still before the multitude, yet without the scribes and Pharisees--He said, "Woman, where are those thine accusers? Hath no man condemned thee? She said, No man, Lord. And Jesus said unto her, Neither do I condemn thee: go, and sin no more."

When we go through an experience like this--I am speaking of the unredeemed, of course--do we stop sinning? Not really, but it does cause our inner man to go past the act to marvel at the wonder of forgiveness. And it is that wonder that often leads to our ultimate repentance where the Lord God can interact in our lives and lead us out of sin.

"How does this story and the sin problem relate to healing, health and wholeness?" you might wish to ask. I'm glad you asked that because if there is no sin, there is no devil; and if there is no devil, there is no sickness or oppression; and if there is no sickness or oppression, there would be no need for this book. So my question is this: "Is your heart, your inner man, totally without sin? Do you believe, whatever your condition, that Jesus condemns you? If He didn't condemn the adulterous woman, why would He condemn you? What worse thing have you done?"

The Word says, "For God sent not His Son into the world to condemn the world; but that the world through Him might be saved" (John 3:17). Further, it tells us if we are condemned that it is our heart that condemns us (1 John 3:20). When? When we do not love or have compassion, according to His commandments, both in deed and in truth. For Jesus said, "A new commandment I give unto you, That ye love one another; as I have loved you, that ye also love one another. By this shall all men know that ye are My disciples, if ye have love one to another" (John 13:34,35).

Not only are we to have love: we are to have perfect love, because the Word says, "There is no fear in love; but perfect love casteth out fear; because fear hath torment [and is the cause of many illnesses and afflictions]. He that feareth is not made perfect [or complete] in love" (1 John 4:18). When we are complete in love, there will be no room for sickness or suffering--for we will be full of God (see I John 3:21-24).

How do we become full of God? Jesus said, "Whatsoever ye shall ask the Father in My Name, He will give it [to] you" (John 16:23). So how about praying this prayer?

Heavenly Father, Your Word says if I ask You anything in the Name of Jesus, You will give it to me. So I'm asking, in the Name that is above every name, the Name of Jesus, to be filled with Your perfect love--that my heart will be as Your heart--that my compassion will be as Your compassion in all things and toward all people. Also Your Word says Your love casts out fear, which brings torment--and which could be the cause of my afflictions. I therefore call to Your remembrance Your promises having to do with love and compassion--that I be able to always be pleasing to You.   *Amen--and Amen*

God so loved . . . that He gave
Read John 3:16

"God so loved . . . that He gave. . . . " We know this as part of the often quoted scripture and we too often regard it in much the same way that we regard breathing--except when we have emphysema-- much too casually. I have to suppose it is because we hear it so often. There is an expression which says, "Familiarity breeds contempt." We see this in our day-to-day vocabulary before we come to know the Lord. I don't know about you but before I was saved, I was always taking the name of God in vain, and it wasn't for lack of a more than adequate vocabulary, as is so often the case. It was because God and Jesus Christ were familiar words and, in their familiarity, and because I was a child of the devil, he led me into using them as curses and expletives.

The reason for setting this forth is to show another facet of God's love and compassion. Looking down the corridor of time to this century; watching knowledge increase and human values diminish (Daniel 12:1-4); seeing sin abound while His grace does much more abound (Romans 5:20); looking to this time when men's hearts are failing them for fear (Luke 21:26); while the righteous are becoming bold as lions (Proverbs 28:1), God knew His Gift of Love would have to encompass (and embrace) all men and all areas of men's lives. You can see this where Jesus tells us, "All manner of sin and blasphemy shall be forgiven unto men: but the blasphemy against the Holy Ghost shall not be forgiven unto men. And whosoever speaketh a word against the Son of man, it shall be forgiven him: but whosoever speaketh a word against the Holy Ghost, it shall not be forgiven him, neither in this world, neither in the world to come" (Matthew 12:31,32).

Isn't that tremendous? The Lord saw that we would one day be guilty of blaspheming Himself and God and so He set up forgiveness in advance. And it must be seen that there is almost no way one can blaspheme the Holy Ghost. It is completely awkward; none of the curses I knew--and you can take my word I knew a lot--were comfortable with "Holy Ghost." Can you imagine anything more gracious for the fool who blasphemes all the time?

The Word further assures us the Holy Spirit (or Holy Ghost) is given only to believers--and usually long before He is comfortably ensconced in our lives we have undergone a thorough heart-scrubbing and mouth-washing. Consider what this does for the unbeliever: it literally keeps him in the position of being forgiven until the time comes for that big decision. Though he may have been baptized (or sprinkled) as a child, which God doesn't consider sufficiently relevant to even mention in the Bible, he wouldn't even have the same standing as the twelve men Paul approached at Ephesus (see Acts 19:1-3) when he (Paul) asked them if they had received the Holy Ghost since they believed. Paul considered them believers, whereas the man in question here--no matter what his denomination--would not be considered a believer. But like the twelve at Ephesus, his confession might be the same. For when the question was put to them, they said, "We have not so much as heard whether there be any Holy Ghost." So obviously you can't blaspheme what you don't know exists--yes? How do you suppose He kept such a dynamic force hidden, especially when He was all the while loving the world?

There are so many areas of our lives to which the Lord wants to have free access. Not in order to control us or our lives with a rod of iron--but so He can step in at any time we have a desperate need.

That is how He wishes to show us His love and compassion. But we have to be open to (and with) Him: that is the first essential. Unless you invite Him in, He will not come; He will not overrule you; nor will He attempt to control your potential. That fact is seen throughout both Testaments. During the forty years in the wilderness, God was continually showing the children of Israel outrageous things for the purpose of revealing Himself and His power and glory. But they rarely acknowledged Him. Even when their "clothes waxed not old, and their feet swelled not" (Nehemiah 9:21), and when they had a continuing supply of manna and water. Phenomenal! But how about you, beloved? Can you daily see His hand in *your* life? It's there, you know.

As the Father hath loved Me
Read John 15:9,10

"As the Father hath loved Me, so have I loved you: continue ye in My love. If ye keep My commandments, ye shall abide in My love; even as I have kept My Father's commandments, and abide in His love." Do you realize that though Jesus came to earth as a man, He never received any of the sin-programmed forms of illness? He was not immune from enemy attack--Satan was freely able to try to put things on Him--but the Word says that though He "was in all points tempted like as we are, yet [He was] without sin."

This is not to make us sin-conscious but to make us aware of the penalties of sin. Once we recognize that Jesus paid every penalty for all sin for all times--past, present and future, for the redeemed as well as the unredeemed--we can go about finding our rights and privileges and appropriate what He has already done for us.

The Bible clearly tells us, "When we were yet without strength, in due time Christ died for the ungodly. For scarcely for a righteous man will one die: yet peradventure for a good man some would even dare to die. But God commendeth His love toward us, in that, while we were yet sinners, Christ died for us" (Romans 5:6-8).

Can you imagine all the garbage of humanity being dumped on the one Man in all the universe who least deserved such a penalty? But that is what happened. He took this ghastly penalty on Himself. The Bible says, "We see Jesus, who was made a little lower than the angels for the suffering of death, crowned with glory and honor; that He by the grace of God should taste death for every man [past, present and future]" (Hebrews 2:9). And to cap off this thought, we read, "Looking unto Jesus the Author and Finisher of our faith; who for the joy that was set before Him [you and me, beloved] endured the cross, despising the shame, and is set down at the right hand of the throne of God" (Hebrews 12:2).

Is there any way you can plumb the depths of such love and compassion as that? If so, you have a better understanding than I do. Frankly, it staggers me.

Could such love be unaware of our sicknesses and pain? The Bible says no. And, of course, we know that Jesus is our Great High Priest: "We have not an high priest which cannot be touched with the feeling of our infirmities" (Hebrews 4:15). When we have an infirmity, we know He feels it.

It is for us then to learn to tap into His perfect love, understanding there is no fear in love--and perfect love casts out fear (1 John 4:18). Could there be any more perfect love than that exhibited by the Lord Jesus? No way. But you, beloved, might have one of those burning questions: "If He feels my infirmities and has perfect love, why doesn't He . . . ?" Countering a question with a question, I ask, "Why don't you?"

After all, He died that dreadful death that you might receive His authority over all sickness, affliction and suffering. That is what His love was mostly all about: giving you His power, while taking on your weakness; becoming "sin for you on the cross, that you might become the righteousness of God in Him"; going into hell for you; defeating Satan in his own territory; taking from him the keys to death and hell so you would not have to undergo the spiritual death that He and the first Adam suffered. There is no greater love than that--the love of God in Christ Jesus our Lord. Can you see that?

As previously pointed out, Jesus said that Satan was a liar, a cheat, a thief and a murderer from the beginning. We recognize that most of these are criminal offenses--for which one is subject to arrest and punishment. However, if we continue to allow his illegal actions to go unpunished he will continue to do them, functioning like the Mafia--with impunity in the face of dereliction of authority.

In order to defeat him and them, we are to be as God described Job to Satan: "Hast thou considered My servant Job, that there is none like him in the earth, a perfect and an upright man, one that feareth God, and escheweth evil?" (Job 1:8). The word *eschew* is a marvelous word in the Hebrew, *sur*, which means "be departed from, go aside from, be revolted by." Also, beloved, it is necessary we remember that our weapons are not carnal, but mighty through God to the pulling down of such strongholds (2 Corinthians 10:4-6). It is a fact that love will prevail: not love for Satan but love for all men, who seeing the love will eschew evil and do good (1 Peter 3:11), thereby overwhelming Satan and the mob. That is the name of the love game.

It was in the prayer room at Georgetown that I first observed the power of compassion and love. It was nothing that I did: it was the love of God in Christ Jesus that would come down in the midst of us. One person right after another would be healed as I felt this surge of love go through and out of me. Sometimes as I merely looked on the people with afflictions, this supernatural love would overwhelm me and almost before I could lay hands on them they would be made whole. No telling what would have happened if I hadn't been so bound by my lack of knowledge of God's healing process. Then again, it may have been because I had no knowledge that the Lord would show Himself by the outpouring of His Love. Who really knows?

There is so much we don't understand, beloved, and I wouldn't say that wasn't a plus where love is concerned, especially if we are

referring to it from an intellectual level. Intellectual love, like the intellectual approach to growing weeds, hasn't got much going for it. If
you have to dissect it to understand and describe it, then there is an
insurmountable problem. If Webster can't do it and the Bible refuses
to do it why not just accept love for what it is--an indescribable
pleasure?

I will love . . . and will manifest Myself to him
Read John 14:21

"I will love . . . and will manifest Myself to him." That is what Jesus
said would happen if we have His commandments and keep them.
He will consider that we love Him--and we that love Him will be
loved of God and He will manifest Himself to us. How do you think
He will do that? Will we see a ghostlike figure or a shade? The few
people I have known, seen or met who have had the Lord manifest
Himself to them have been very stable people of international reputation.

Personally, I expect to see the Lord in the flesh--for He is in the
flesh, you know--before I am caught up to be with Him forever. He
knows that is the desire of my heart. But we can understand that
isn't the only way He can manifest Himself. Because He said of Himself when He appeared in their midst (after His death, burial and
resurrection), and His disciples were terrified, "Why are ye troubled?
and why do thoughts arise in your hearts? Behold My hands and My
feet, that it is I Myself: handle Me and see; for a spirit hath not flesh
and bone, as ye see Me have" (see Luke 24:36-39). Further, Jesus
said, "And, lo, I am with you alway, even unto the end of the world"
(Matthew 28:20) and the Mark account says, "And they went forth,
and preached every where, the Lord working with them, and confirming the word with signs following" (Mark 16:20).

Those of us who have healing ministries know that without His
being with us always and working with us, confirming His Word with
signs following, we would forever be wondering whether tonight is
the night or whether this is the time. All of us are aware that we

aren't always blessed with a physical, seeable, touchable, hearable manifestation of His presence. But we know unalterably that when signs and wonders are taking place, it is because He is there--and certainly not because we are in any way special. It is because of His infinite love and compassion; it is because we are present and usable; and it is because there is not a great shadow of doubt hanging over the place (see Matthew 13:54-58).

It is not for us to speculate on what He will do *when*; how He will manifest Himself and to whom; where His presence will be felt the strongest. All such things are in His keeping. Only He knows what to do to whom--how, when, why and where.

Some of you might wonder in your hearts, saying, "Since I don't have any way to know these things, I could be left out." But no, that is not what He says. He says you are to have and keep His commandments. Thus He will know that you love Him, that you will be loved of Him and the Father and that He will have free access to manifesting Himself in, through and to you--at which point you will not have to wonder about anything. You will be whole.

Few of us spend nearly enough time in praise and worship and in the giving of thanks for the manifested presence of God in our lives every day. The Word says that Jesus is "the true Light that lighteth every man that cometh into the world" (John 1:8,9). He is the light of life without which we are physically and spiritually dead. We breathe, our hearts beat, our brains function--we see, feel, hear, taste, touch, smell--because of the manifested love of God. And everything we see, feel, hear, taste, touch and smell--everything that moves and grows and has a life cycle--is part and parcel of the manifested love of God.

One of the most unique approaches to the love of God is on a record called "Sonshiny Day," by Ken Medema, blind piano artist, composer and singer. Paraphrasing what it says: "Love taught the flowers how to grow; love taught the rivers how to flow; love taught the eagle how to fly; love taught the rain clouds how to pour; love taught the thunder how to roar; love made the mountains touch the

sky; love made the early morning mine; love made the moon and
stars to shine." Isn't that wonderful?

Until the Spirit-filled believer becomes conscious of God inside
him, it is difficult for him to know what His love does in them or
through them. But once that time comes, Jesus says, "At that day ye
shall know that I am in My Father, and ye in Me, and I in you" (John
14:20).

Oh, beloved, how very important it is for us to know that God
abides in us so we can say, like David, "Thou art my hiding place;
Thou shalt preserve me from trouble; Thou shalt compass me about
with songs of deliverance. Selah" (Psalm 32:7). Then God can pick
up the ball, as He does: "I will instruct thee and teach thee in the way
which thou shalt go: I will guide thee with Mine eye. Be ye not as the
horse, or as the mule, which have no understanding: whose mouth
must be held in with bit and bridle, lest they come near unto thee.
Many sorrows shall be to the wicked: but he that trusteth in the
Lord, mercy shall compass him about. Be glad in the Lord, and rejoice, ye righteous: and shout for joy, all ye that are upright in heart"
(Psalm 32:8-11). If you tie all this together with Colossians 3:1-3 and
Romans 8:1,2, you will see a vital truth that will make you every whit
whole--if you believe.

To paraphrase briefly, we know that though our bodies still live,
we are crucified--dead and buried with Christ--and that being so,
that we are also risen with Him. Therefore we are to seek and think
on those things which are above, not on things of the earth. If, then,
"ye are dead, and your life is hid with Christ in God" (Colossians
3:3), how can any live affliction flourish in you? The truth is, it
can't--unless you allow it.

This is not meant to put anyone who is sick under condemnation, for "There is therefore now no condemnation to them which
are in Christ Jesus, who walk not after the flesh, but after the Spirit.
For the law of the Spirit of life in Christ Jesus hath made me free
from the law of sin and death" (Romans 8:1,2). Can you see that?
Nothing like arthritis, rheumatism, ulcers, heart trouble, high blood

pressure or cancer can have any effect on a dead body. That is why we must reckon ourselves dead indeed unto sin, but alive unto God through Jesus Christ our Lord (Romans 6:11).

How about praying a prayer much like this?

Lord God, there are so many mysteries in Your Word--things I long to understand but don't. I know You have assured me I have Your wisdom, but I don't have the foggiest notion how to reckon myself dead. Though I can give mental assent to such statements, Father, I don't know how to apply them in my day-to-day life, knowing my heart is beating and my general bodily functions continuing. So I ask, Lord God, that You grant me, according to Your riches in glory, the knowledge that I am strengthened with might by Your Spirit in my inner man, that Your faith dwells in my heart, and that I am rooted and grounded in Your love. So that all You desire of me in knowing and understanding how I participated with the Lord Jesus in His death, burial and resurrection may be accomplished and that I can be dead to everything that is in opposition to You. All this I ask in Jesus' Name.

Amen--and Amen

He hath no form or comeliness
Read Isaiah 53:2

"He hath no form or comeliness; and when we shall see him, there is no beauty that we should desire Him." Isaiah wrote this somewhere around 712 B.C. And, of course, he was writing about Christ. This was nearly 700 years before Christ was even born. Yet the last three verses of chapter 52 and all of 53 give us a graphic picture of the Lord Jesus' beating, crucifixion, death, trial and victory in hell, His resurrection and ascension--even His vision of us--down to the very last detail. Similarly, we see astonishing Messianic passages in Psalm 22, written and sung by King David as much as a thousand years before Christ. The Lord God gave the prophets visions of the future they had no way of interpreting with understanding: they just knew these were visions from God and that it was necessary for them to be set forth. Unless the Lord specifically told them, I doubt if they knew there would one day be a book called the Bible and that what they were writing or having written was for you and me two-to-four thousand years later.

As we gather together the Messianic passages from Isaiah 53 and Psalm 22, not only does the Lord Jesus emerge triumphant but so do we--as the righteous children of promise. Could any greater love be shown anywhere by anyone?

Beloved, could a love that was willing to endure such torture and pain for you, personally, be oblivious to your suffering and torment now--even to that relentless ugliness that seems to be dragging you toward death? No, we are the joy that was set before Him, the reason He was willing to endure the cross (Hebrews 12:2). Would such a love, after going through this gross and bitter experience, throw in the sponge? Of course not. He didn't sweat blood in the Garden of Gethsemane (Luke 22:44) as a sort of dramatic gesture to prepare you for what was to come. He knew precisely, to the last gruesome detail, what was to happen to Him.

As Jesus was giving Himself up to the soldiers of the high priest, Peter drew his sword and smote Malchus, cutting off his ear. Jesus rebuked Peter, saying, "Put up again thy sword into his place: for all they that take the sword shall perish with the sword" (Matthew 26:52). Then He says something that gives us a true picture of His position with the Father: "Thinkest thou that I cannot now pray to My Father, and He shall presently give me more than twelve legions [possibly as many as 60,000] of angels? But how then shall the scriptures be fulfilled, that thus it must be?" (Matthew 26:53,54).

If one angel can destroy all of Jerusalem (2 Samuel 24:16), we can see that 60,000 could have taken the entire Middle East. But it was necessary that the Lord suffer indescribable torments so that we wouldn't have to, that the scriptures be fulfilled (see Psalm 22: 22-31).

Though the gospels don't tell us in detail, the beginning words of this segment show us a portrait of the Savior most of us don't see. He was not a puny, sad-faced weakling hanging there on the cross. He was the Son of man, who had been stripped naked, beaten and pommeled nearly beyond recognition. He was then crowned with thorns, and a purple robe (of royalty), was put on Him to ridicule Him. While Pilate's soldiers were doing this, they were saying, "Hail, King of the Jews"--after which they again smote Him with their hands (see Matthew 26:57-68; Mark 14:55-65; Luke 22:54-65; John 18:12--19:3).

But worse than the beatings, the buffeting, the pommeling, the moral torments of ridicule and derision, there was the separation from the Father. Nothing was so terrible for Christ as the aggregate of all the sin of all mankind being poured out on Him. Because God cannot look on sin, He, therefore, could not even look on His beloved Son (see Habakkuk 1:12,13). Though there are those who would have Christ quoting Psalm 22:1 from the cross while hanging there in terrifying agony, His back looking like raw hamburger, His hands and feet pierced with nails the size of railroad spikes, gasping for breath, slowly bleeding to death--nothing paralleled the intense anguish of being unable to reach God. You see, in all the centuries and millennia that He was with the Father, they were never before apart. Now here He was in the agony of torment, hanging there in excruciating pain, separated from His heavenly Father, knowing He had to go into hell and endure even more distress and humiliation. How could He undergo such suffering--and to what end? Would you believe He did that for us? That is what He did for the joy that was set before Him--you and me.

And, as for Psalm 22:1: David was quoting Him; He was not quoting David. For when David wrote Psalm 22--a thousand years before Christ was born--he was writing under the inspiration of the Holy Spirit, who was creating a scripture for Jesus to fulfill. And why did He create the situation? So we could see the truth and be made healthy and whole of whatever is bothering us. What love He has toward us! "My Lord and my God!" Thomas uttered in amazement (John 20:28).

For you who have the same difficulty grasping the vastness of such a love, I suggest this prayer:

Holy Father, I call on You this day to be El Shaddai, the all-sufficient One, the One who is more than enough, the One who surpasses the natural and allows us access to the supernatural, the One who blesses beyond what man can imagine. And I thank You, God, that You have allowed me to enter Your gates with thanksgiving and come into Your courts with praise. There is no power like Your power, there is no force like Your force, there is no love like Your love and compassion. So as I come before Your throne of grace this day, I come with the awe and wonder of a little child, knowing I have found favor in Your sight--knowing beyond the shadow of a doubt that You have given me everything that is my due. But Father, I remind You that I am unalterably human and, therefore, fallible. I am staggered at the knowledge of what Your unfailing love has accomplished in and through me, that I am everything You have assured me I am and that I have enough love and compassion to cover the earth with blessings. So I ask You by Your Spirit in my inner man to show me how to use all that You have given me--and to use it as You use it. All this I ask in Jesus' Name.   *Amen--and Amen*

The kingdom of God is come upon you
Read Luke 11:20,21

"The kingdom of God is come upon you," Jesus said. But He also said, "The kingdom of God cometh not with observation: neither shall ye say, Lo here! or, lo there! for, behold, the kingdom of God is within you" (Luke 17:20,21). Then He tells us, "Verily I say unto you, Whosoever shall not receive the kingdom of God as a little child shall in no wise enter therein" (Luke 18:17).

How do little children receive anything good? With awe and wonder? with great glee and clapping of hands? with innocent rejoicing? Do they have grateful hearts? What do you suppose the Lord had in mind when He made that statement? What are we to surmise, or what action should we take to ensure that we are in compliance? I don't remember ever reading anything in the Bible that served as a suitable explanation. But in observing children and how they receive gifts of toys and other playthings, I have noticed that first moment of surprised delight, followed shortly by playing with it on the floor, taking it apart, hitting their little brother with it, then going on to something else. So how does this relate to receiving the kingdom as they should, would or could?

In making my point on receiving as a little child, I have used some levity, I know. But that was merely a device to get your attention focused on where I am headed. Now you can watch as I shift gears to get over the next hill and down into the valley of loving innocence. It is there we will see the ultimate comparisons.

In the plains of Serengeti and the Ngora Ngora Crater in East Africa, hundreds of thousands of different animals live in innocent harmony until the stomachs of the predators begin to growl with hunger. Then there is a cautious uneasiness among the herds. Zebras, gazelles, wildebeests, water bucks, kudus--even the giant water buffaloes--become fidgety and apprehensive. There is much tail-twitching and looking over shoulders.

Suddenly, from out of nowhere comes a lioness, or a cheetah, or wild dogs and (sometimes) a leopard. The scramble is on--the prey scatters in terror. You see the mad dash, the brief chase and the kill. In seconds, it is over and in moments there is the return to innocence. Nothing out of the ordinary, nothing amiss--it is just the way things are.

But that isn't how God meant for it to be: that isn't the way He made it in the beginning. It was His intention that the wolf and the lamb should feed together, and the lion and the bullock should eat straw together (see Isaiah 65:25). However, when Satan deceived

Adam and Eve, thus taking away Adam's dominion over the earth (because of their disobedience), he perverted every good and perfect thing God had made and had them conform to his evil purposes. As a consequence, the predator; and as a consequence, childish violence. Just as the battle, so the peace. All things follow a pattern--regardless of when and where established and by whom.

Certainly there would be few of us who haven't seen children playing together in innocent harmony, much as the previously described animals. One moment they are quietly participating in some game or watching in fascination as a wasp and a spider fight it out in a jar. The next moment they are joyously romping about with shouts of laughter and running and leaping together, only to wind up the next moment in a battle for supremacy, with the younger being knocked around by the elder. Then after the hurt feelings are soothed and the bruises forgotten, there is the return to innocent harmony, just as though nothing had ever happened.

What does all this have to do with receiving the kingdom of God as a little child? These examples were set forth to show that pretty much all living things act and/or react according to their nature as long as their nature hasn't been changed by receiving the Lord Jesus Christ as Savior and Lord. As long as that nature remains under the dominion of Satan, it will conform to his authority and control. That is how the curse of the law continues to plague the unredeemed and how he influences the thinking and the emotions of those unfortunates. He tells them that God put their sicknesses on them so if they quietly suffer the pain and consequences, He will be exalted and those afflicted raised up, which is, of course, deception.

That is among the many reasons Jesus defeated Satan and gave us His Spirit, so we would have Jesus' discernment and dominion; so we would know how to deal with the lies Satan has perpetrated over the centuries; so we could know the God of love and peace and, in the knowing, come to know that where peace and harmony reign supreme, there is no sickness and pain. And that is God's purpose: that we have His peace.

Despite the occasional turmoil, misunderstandings and minor bloodletting, children are basically at peace with themselves and enjoy universal harmony. And their innocence is at once astonishing and charming as long as we don't burden them with more responsibility than their natures allow. You see, the kingdom of God brings no burdens. In fact, it comes to carry your burdens and to take away your sorrows and suffering, because it is Jesus who brings the kingdom (see Luke 17; Isaiah 53).

The kingdom comes in innocence and it seeks its own, which are the children. As their motives are basically pure, so are they of the kingdom. The kingdom is within you only for your good: it doesn't benefit God, nor will it do very much for you if you don't learn why it is there and how you are to live in it.

"Seek ye first the kingdom of God, and His righteousness [within you]; and all these things will be added unto you" (Matthew 6:33), the Word says. Healing, health and wholeness are within you: love, joy, peace and plenty are within your grasp; and above all, Christ and God and the Holy Spirit are there to guide and lead you into all truth--as well as to sustain you in every godly endeavor. Isn't that tremendous!

Here you might wish to say a prayer of affirmation that would go like this:

Father of all glory and righteousness, the Lord God of peace and harmony, the Almighty who is the essence of love and compassion, who is the possessor of heaven and earth, who has deigned to place Your kingdom within me, I thank You for the revelation of Your Presence and Your loving righteousness within me as well. I know that You have done all things well, according to Your Word (Mark 7:37) and I rejoice that You have made me healthy and whole. Because, Father, I now see that unless I allow it, Satan has no place in me. So by the authority You have given me through Jesus Christ the Lord, I now accept the healing You have so graciously given me and will neither receive or acknowledge

*any form of oppression the evil one will attempt to put on me.
For I am totally and unalterably free of all bondage. Hallelujah
to Jesus--and glory to His Name--by which I pray.*

Amen--and Amen

8

Healing, Health and Wholeness
By Two Agreeing on Earth

If two of you shall agree
Read Matthew 18:18-20

"If two of you shall agree . . . " As you probably know, this is a portion of the dynamic threesome--the three scriptures Jesus exhorted
us to apply in our day-to-day living: "Verily I say unto you, Whatsoever ye shall bind on earth shall be bound in heaven: and whatsoever ye shall loose on earth shall be loosed in heaven. Again I say
unto you, That if two of you shall agree on earth as touching any
thing that they shall ask, it shall be done for them of My Father
which is in heaven. For where two or three are gathered together in
My Name, there am I in the midst of them."

If you are already using these scriptures, I say, "Glory to God"
and "Amen." But for you who have not yet received the power revelation resident in these scriptures, I say, "Hold onto your hats--for
surely you will soon be in shouting Holy Ghost territory."

Before we get into breaking this down, however, you ought to
see Matthew 16:13-19. To paraphrase, Jesus asked His disciples,
"Who do men say that I the Son of man am?" One said John the Baptist, another said Elijah and still another said Jeremiah. "But," Jesus
asked, "who say *ye* that I am?" Then the precipitous Peter said,
"Thou art the Christ, the Son of the living God." The next verses go
on to say, "And Jesus answered and said unto him, Blessed art thou,
Simon Bar-jonah: for flesh and blood hath not revealed it unto thee,
but My Father which is in heaven. And I say also unto thee, That

thou art Peter [Greek *petros*, "a piece of rock"], and upon this rock
[Greek *petra*, "a mass of rock," speaking of Himself as the Christ of
God] I will build My church; and the gates of hell shall not prevail
against it. And I will give unto thee [the Church] the keys of the
kingdom of heaven: and whatsoever thou shalt bind on earth shall be
bound in heaven: and whatsoever thou shalt loose on earth shall be
loosed in heaven" (Matthew 16:17-19).

Matthew 18:18 is nearly a direct copy of the last part of 16:19.
In 16:19, Jesus is referring to His Church receiving the keys to the
kingdom of heaven, and in 18:18 He is instructing the church on how
they are to regard children and new converts and how they are to
govern disagreements among the brethren.

In order to understand the "rock" sequence, it is vital for us to
grasp the significance of Matthew 16:13-19. Numerous scriptures
portray Jesus as the Rock: Exodus 17:1-7; Numbers 20:8-11;
2 Samuel 22:2-4; Psalms 31:3; 78:16; Matthew 16:18; Romans 9:33;
and I Corinthians 10:4, which sums them all up. I would that all
believers would find out the significance of having their faith and
trust in God founded on Christ, the solid Rock (Luke 6:48). For
when they do, it is impossible for that faith to be shaken or destroyed by the storms and floods of life. As a result, we never have
the horrendous mess or clean-up of the aftermath.

But back to the dynamic threesome. We will be dealing with
binding and loosing (Matthew 18:18) in a later section of this chapter. At this point, I want to show you something interesting about "If
two of you shall agree. . . . "

Here the Greek word for *agree* is *sumphoneo*, which means "to
agree, agree together or agree with"--but the implication (because of
the second and third syllable, *phoneo*) is "to agree together out loud."
When we tie this to the root word, *sumphonia*, meaning "music"--and
its counterpart, *sumphonesis*, which is "concord" (or "harmony"), we
have the concept of a perfectly harmonious symphony.

When we consider the power built into this little five-letter
word, *agree*, we can see we are dealing in some pretty heavy stuff.

Meditate on what the Lord Jesus is saying here: "If two of you shall agree on earth . . . " Unless you are in a plane, balloon or dirigible, anyone reading this is certainly on the earth--or soon will be. Jesus' exhortation here is crystal clear as are the two principal requirements: we must be in agreement and we must be on earth. Beyond these basic requirements, it is my opinion that two being in agreement has more than ordinary significance. I have heard many pastors, teachers and laymen set forth a problem or motion for prayer before the body of Christ by saying, "Let's all agree . . . " That just isn't wisdom (in light of the scripture), unless the agreement is absolutely concise and unable to be altered. Otherwise, the Lord Jesus would have said, "If a host of you shall agree . . . " Do you see what I am getting at?

As an example: one evening in the prayer room, a woman came forward with a request. She wanted to stand in proxy for a member of her family who was soon to be going to the hospital for a serious operation. Since, up to this time, we had great success with the prayer of agreement, I thought to use it on this particular evening in this circumstance. But what a fiasco! And what a lesson!

There were five or six others on the platform with me. Wishing to involve them and being ignorant of the importance of the numbers in agreement, I said "Let's all agree . . . " Then I stood back and listened instead of participating as I usually did. Until this moment, it had never occurred to me that the Lord had said, "If *two* of you shall agree . . . " And it was in this experience that I learned there is no such thing as a casual remark in any of Jesus' teachings or exhortations. For as I stood back and listened, I heard: "Lord, heal her right where she is" and "Lord, heal her in the ambulance on the way to the hospital" and "Let the doctors not find anything wrong" and "Let everything go off smoothly, so she can be a witness to everybody in the hospital."

Can you see that the Lord wouldn't be able to honor any of these prayers? What we did was try to build a foundation on agreement without establishing *what we were to agree about*. And what could be more important in an agreement than to have something to agree on?

If you have an occasion to seek the Lord's blessing through an agreement in prayer, it is essential to find some *one* person to agree with you. Be explicit about what you need or desire--and as simply concise as possible. God loves you and greatly desires to answer your prayers and supplications. But keep in mind that He knows those prayers that tend to ramble all over the countryside are rarely offered in faith and are almost never said while believing the answer has already been given (see Mark 11:24 again).

A prayer focused on the "agreement key" might go something like this:

Father in heaven, I see the importance of what the Lord Jesus had to say concerning two people agreeing on earth. Also, Father, I see how Your boundless grace is involved in the answers to those prayers of agreement. To agree with me, Lord, I need exactly the right people--with wisdom and understanding--who will not thwart our purposes, my God. By Your Spirit, I ask that You guide and lead me in the kind of prayers You can answer--and that I be made sensitive to those brothers and sisters who will have understanding of Your Word and Your purposes for me and them. This I ask in Jesus' Name. Also, Father, I want to be taught how and when I can enter the prayer of agreement with the Lord Jesus. For while I know He is seated at Your right hand in heaven, I also know He is on earth as well--for Your Word assures me that He is in You and in me [John 14:19,20]. Now, Father, I thank You that I have my answer--as I call those things that be not as though they are--just as You do.   Amen--and Amen

There am I in the midst
Read Matthew 18:19,20

In the very next verse after "If two of you shall agree . . . ," Jesus says, "For where two or three are gathered together in My Name, there am I in the midst of them." This in no way negates what was said about two agreeing, but it does make it easy to see how people are guilty of misquoting scriptures, saying things like, "For the Bible says, if two or three agree . . . " In truth, however, it says no such thing. It says, "If two of you shall agree . . . " and "Where two or three are gathered together. . . . "

It may seem to you that I am splitting hairs but I truly am not. What I am doing is emphasizing the importance of obedience to the Word--not just vaguely assenting to what we think. For I believe it is possible for two, ten or even a thousand to agree--if they can be confined to specifics without wavering. But the greater the number involved, the less the likelihood of agreement. Hosts of people are just not all that staunch in mass unshakableness.

As is indicated by the preceding prayer, when there is no one visible around to agree with, it is possible to have the Lord agree with you. And who would be a better informed and more reliable partner? But we must be very wary here. For it is easy for the person seeking agreement to be out of the realm where God can be in agreement.

God can never agree with anything that violates His Word, which is His will. For instance, asking the Lord to agree with you that He will heal so-and-so is in direct opposition to His Word which says He has already healed them. In effect, what is being said is, "I don't believe Your Word, God, but I want You to agree anyway." Can you see that?

Another intriguing truth couched in verse twenty is this: Jesus being in the midst of us doesn't assure anything more than His Presence. "How can that be?" you might ask. *Why would He bother to come?* you might wonder. I say He is with us to watch over His Word to perform it (Jeremiah 1:12). And what a remarkable revelation that is! Think of it: Jesus, the Lord of heaven and earth, the King of kings and Lord of lords, loving us enough to come and be with us where two or three of us are gathered together in His Name, simply to see that our scriptural prayers are answered. This doesn't imply that He doesn't answer other prayers of the heart: I have seen Him do it at times--much to my astonishment. But given all the options, He can do as He wills or sees fit. Question: Have you given Him all the options?

There are numbers of recorded incidents where someone went into a sick room to pray for a person, only to see the Lord Jesus standing there in the room, seemingly doing nothing but just standing there.

In a book I read recently, a woman told of having a vision of being transported with great speed across the sea and into a hospital room, there to see a woman she assumed to have cancer. To her complete surprise, she saw Jesus standing in the corner of the room. She went over and knelt before Him and asked what she should do. The Lord simply said, "Pray for her," which she did.

Why do you suppose the Lord didn't do it Himself, since He was right there? Why didn't He just go ahead and manifest her healing? Could it possibly be that you and I are to be the Jesus here on the earth--we, His Body? I believe there is no time when He is not doing what is necessary, even if only watching over His Word to perform it (see also Philippians 1:6).

Dr. Kenneth Hagin has had numerous visions of the Lord, one of which is particularly appropriate here. It seems he and another fellow were in the middle of a large stadium when they saw two ferocious lions rushing toward them. His companion immediately fled, leaving Kenneth trembling with fear. Since he felt escape was impossible, he just stood there, not knowing what to do. Then, looking over his shoulder, he saw the Lord Jesus standing there with His arms folded apparently unwilling to do anything to help. Wondering why the Lord wasn't doing anything--and not knowing what to do himself--he remained frozen in his tracks. When he didn't move, however, the lions slowed to a stop in front of him, sniffed around his feet and trotted off.

Were the lions real or were they just a part of the vision? And which is the more frightening, the real or the imaginary? What I am getting at, beloved, is that dreams, visions and nightmares--at least those that are hairy and scary--are things the Lord is not likely to do anything about. Why? Because He has already given us instructions in His Word about how to deal with them. Like vain imaginations and anything else that exalts itself above the knowledge of God (2 Corinthians 10:5), they are to be cast down.

Fear not only brings torment, quite literally putting us under the authority of the tormentor, Satan, it stands like an impenetrable cloud between the Lord and ourselves (1 John 4:18; Romans 8:15). Where we know we are to have faith in order to please God, we should be equally aware that Satan's substitute is fear. If Satan can keep you in bondage to fear, you cannot possibly have the faith to be healed, healthy and whole--because faith and fear cannot co-exist in any situation. They are like hot and cold water: one neutralizes the other. If you combine hot faith and cold fear, the best you can come up with is warm or cool. And in healing, health and wholeness, that just isn't good enough.

What we need to know in our hearts, what we need to understand through the renewing of our minds and what we need to experience through our spiritual growth is the Emmanuel effect, the God-with-us-no-matter-what condition.

Not only is He with us in a two-or-more situation to watch over His Word to perform it, He is with us in every action and circumstance, whether in joy or sorrow, peace or turmoil, abundance or poverty, health or affliction. The Word says that He is our high priest and that He rejoices in our rejoicing and that He is touched with the feeling of our infirmities. The way He can experience our every emotion and feeling and understand our every desire and need is to be with us in every situation and circumstance.

All of us have heard of horrendous tragedies that have happened across the world from us. And the best most of us could muster in the way of compassion would be a brief "Tsk, tsk," or perhaps a shrug of helplessness. But if we had been on the scene, how much more vivid our responses would have been! When you comprehend that distinction between hearing a brief news report and actually being there when it happens, you can immediately comprehend the difference between God being way out there somewhere and the God of all glory being within you. Yes, that is the Immanuel effect (see Isaiah 7:14; 8:8). And it is this depth of understanding in our hearts or inner man that gives us confidence in what the Word says we are--and therefore absolute victory over the enemy--making us more than conquerors instead of the vanquished.

In order to wholly cooperate with the Word of God--knowing that He died for us and arose for us so that we might enjoy every God-ordained benefit--we might here use a prayer of profession (or confession) of faith:

I thank You, Lord God, that You have made me to be Your wis-dom, Your righteousness, Your sanctification and Your redemp-tion. I thank You that Your Word says that no weapon formed against me shall prosper; that You are the strength of my life so that I need not be afraid; that I need not fear, because Your love has been shed abroad in my heart; that because Your Word is truth I can have all confidence that every good thing and every per-fect thing is mine through Christ Jesus, my Lord. Also I am grate-ful, Father, that I don't have to search for human solutions to all these things, that You have declared them to be gifts--gifts of love from Your great heart. What a wonder You are, Lord God, and how merciful and generous. How truly Your glory shines through every lovingkindness! I thank You also that You are big enough to have overcome the world--and yet are intimate enough to share my concerns and hear my prayers. Glory, glory, Lord God Al-mighty.   *Amen--and Amen*

Agree with thine adversary quickly
Read Matthew 5:25

As a part of the Sermon on the Mount, Jesus says, "Agree with thine adversary quickly, whiles thou art in the way with him; lest at any time thine adversary deliver thee to the judge, and the judge deliver thee to the officer, and thou be cast into prison." This scripture bothered me for a long while. Can you see why? My concern was, of course, "What if my adversary is the devil? Why should I agree with him at all, much less quickly? And why would I ever be 'in the way' with him?"

But knowing the Lord is never wrong, as I meditated on this scripture and those around it, I knew I had to be missing something. So I prayed, "Lord, under what circumstances should I agree or walk with my adversary, especially if he happens to be Satan? This is a biggie, Lord, and I covet Your input here. Your Word says the steps of a good man are ordered by You and You delight in his ways [Psalm 37:23]. And it doesn't say anything about either agreeing with or walking with my enemy in the way. So? . . . "

Questioning the Lord in this way might seem presumptuous to you. But it is my opinion the Lord not only wants us to question His Word--with the idea of gaining a fuller understanding--but to have the deepest possible insight into its meanings and instructions. Keep in mind the Lord wants to have an intimate relationship with us--not only in our thoughts but in our lives. But how can we properly respond to His desires if we have great gaps in our understanding of His character and nature?

You surely know the devil is not about to agree with you in the matter of healing, health and wholeness. So whatever can be the implication of this scripture? Do you know? Do you care? Are you even curious? I surely was.

Having put it before the Lord in prayer, considering it a need to know and knowing He will supply all my need according to His riches in glory, I rested in His promise. Then one morning I asked a young minister for his understanding of that scripture. His explanation was so simple and concise that I was embarrassed at not having seen it myself. "Goodness, Lord," I said, "what a numbskull I've been! Why couldn't I see that?"

He didn't find it necessary to answer.

As you quite possibly know, the devil often attacks us through some form of condemnation, trying to keep us in bondage to something we have done wrong. Satan might come at you with some accusation like, "You're never going to get your healing (or your prayers answered, or whatever). You remember that argument you had with your wife/husband and those nasty things you said?" It is here that you can agree with your adversary quickly: "Yes, Satan, I know I have sinned, being in strife. But I went before the Lord God and I repented and asked His forgiveness right after I had asked my wife's/husband's forgiveness. And, it is written, 'if we confess our sins, he is faithful and just to forgive us our sins, and to cleanse us from all unrighteousness' [1 John 1:9]. So I'm as pure as the driven snow. Therefore, get lost, you foul thing, in Jesus' Name."

Even if you have been in strife or contention--or in any one of the tremendous number of sins available to us--the solution is the same. Confess your sin or sins to the Father, who is faithful and just to forgive your sins. If you haven't yet taken your sins before Him because, for whatever reason, you feel justified and now your heart is condemning you and you don't know why, the solution remains the same: Go before Him and confess. For the Word says, "And hereby we know that we are of the truth, and shall assure our hearts before Him. For if our heart condemn us, God is greater than our heart, and knoweth all things. Beloved, if our heart condemn us not, then have we confidence toward God. And whatsoever we ask, we receive of Him, because we keep His commandments, and do those things that are pleasing in His sight" (1 John 3:19-22).

Can you see that we cannot afford the luxury of self-righteousness?

Repent ye, and believe the gospel
Read Mark 1:15

"Repent ye, and believe the gospel," Jesus said as He was preaching to the people of Galilee. He prefaced this instruction with these words: "The time is fulfilled, and the kingdom of God is at hand."

Are you sufficiently aware that the kingdom of God is at hand--
especially you who are in need of healing, health and wholeness?
Are you blocking the road to your own healing? After all, if the
kingdom of God is indeed at hand, and Jesus makes that quite clear,
and more importantly, if the kingdom of God is in you, and Jesus
makes that equally clear (Luke 17:21), how dare you be so blatantly
ignorant of our privileges in Him?

If any reader is sick or afflicted in his/her spirit, soul or body,
remember that God has not the smallest lack: He knows every detail
of cause and effect; He has all wisdom and knowledge of your every
need; and He has all the power (Greek, *dunamis*) necessary to make
you completely whole. If you are a born-again, Spirit-filled believer--
which makes you His child--can there be any doubt as to His love or
intentions toward you? Obviously, He wants only the best for you.
Could there be any other purpose in His loving heart than to bless
you? Could He who knows the end from the beginning be guilty of
testing you with sickness to see how strong you are if He already
knows the answer? Goodness!

Most of our problems stem from the desire to bring God down
to a level just a hair's breadth above us. Is that ever a trap! When we
get into this kind of thinking we begin to rationalize away the power
of God by taking a small scrap of His mantle and draping it over the
shoulders of some poor, unsuspecting physician or surgeon. Of
course there is nothing wrong with having confidence in doctors and
hospitals. But before going to them, did you first go to God the
Father? And did you go in the Name of Jesus?

In seeking healing, too often Christians try to justify going to
doctors by saying (defiantly), "Well, God made doctors, didn't He?"
The answer is, "Of course He did. But He also made the chipmunk
and the blue whale--and you and me." But that only proves God is
outrageously versatile and limitless in His multiformity. So when you
suffer an affliction as a Christian and you don't first seek the goodness, mercy and wisdom of God, the chipmunk or the blue whale
might be the best next bet. When you involve God through prayer

and supplication, He gives all the grace and lovingkindness to the enterprise--seeing to it that the wrong doctor is on vacation, the wrong hospital is too busy--making your way arrow-straight.

You can see, beloved, when either through vanity or ignorance we diminish God's towering strength in our own lives by diverting His purposes or misappropriating His Word, that we miss so very much. You might be wondering how a puny little man can diminish God's strength or divert His purposes. I say to you, it is as simple as throwing a piece of metal across a live wire. You know that will cause a short circuit and immediately cut off the power beyond that point. But you also realize that your action doesn't affect the power plant, which goes right on generating the same amount of power to all its other customers on a business-as-usual basis.

It is much the same with God. You can short-circuit your own supply--except where His overriding grace causes a circuit bypass essential for His purposes--but you can't diminish God's overall power supply to all mankind. Like the power company, He, too, works on a business-as-usual basis. Only instead of supplying a community, county or state, He supplies the whole world, including the power plant. He really is a very big God, much, much bigger than we can possibly comprehend.

I recently read an article called "The Open Space in the North." It told about a thrilling discovery astronomers (not astrologists) have made concerning a great empty space in the north in the nebula (which Webster describes as "a large class of celestial structures, of great extension and extreme tenuity, composed of matter in a gaseous or finely divided state") of the constellation of Orion. It is so gigantic the mind of man cannot possibly comprehend it--and so brilliantly beautiful that there are no words to adequately describe it. It is nearly seventeen trillion miles in diameter (17,000,000,000,000). Our earth's orbit is less than 200,000,000 miles, which means that Orion is 90,000 times that size. Thirty thousand solar systems the size of ours (with a sun and moon in the midst of each) wouldn't reach across the opening. Yet God made it by the power of His spoken word, saying, "Let there be . . . "

When one considers the billions of believers who will occupy heaven--with each having a mansion prepared for us by Jesus Christ Himself (John 14:1-3)--we see that such a nebula could be the location of the mount of the congregation, in the sides of the north referred to in Isaiah 14:13. The article further suggested that Job might have had a revelation when he said of God: "He stretcheth out the north over the empty place, and hangeth the earth upon nothing" (Job 26:7). How awesome is His power, might and dominion in heaven and earth! And to think it can be utterly negated in the individual life by doubt and unbelief. Preposterous? The Bible tells us that is the way it is.

So what is our answer? One of our great contemporary Bible teachers tells us, "Don't doubt the Bible: doubt your doubts." And another exhortation to consider is this: When the thief (Satan) comes to steal away your faith and confidence, you can tell him, "God said it; Jesus did it; I believe it--and that settles it." If he then challenges you, saying, "Can you give me chapter and verse on that?" you can say, "Of course. God said it from cover to cover; and Jesus did it from cover to cover; and I believe it from cover to cover; and that settles it forever and ever. Amen."

Rivers of living water
Read John 7:37,38

Is there a born-again, Spirit-filled believer among us who doesn't thirst after more of God? I can't imagine it. But the problem is--at least when we are suffering trials and afflictions--we don't confidently know what to do or how to find out. But God didn't create us out of an unsearchable love only to hide His purposes in obscurity. He generously put His Word in our hearts (or inward parts, as in Job 38:31-41); and then He gave us His written word to confirm it. As if that weren't enough, He gave us His Living Word, the Lord

Jesus, as visible proof and to be the fulfillment (in the flesh) of all
He had said and done.

In two of the places where Jesus said, "Come unto Me . . . "
(Matthew 11:28-30; John 7:37,38), the message is the same, even
though the results differ. According to the Matthew scripture, if you
are struggling with your problems and are burdened down with your
oppressions and afflictions, when you come to Him, He gives you
rest for your spirit, soul and body. As you are yoked together with
Him and walk with Him, He takes all your heaviness onto His side
of the yoke, thereby freeing you up to get in step with Him. The two
of you can walk together because you are agreed (Amos 3:3).

The whole thrust here is centered around the free flow of
God's goodness, mercy and grace. And it is the same in the scripture
in John: "In the last day, that great day of the feast, Jesus stood and
cried, saying, If any man thirst, let him come unto Me, and drink. He
that believeth on Me, as the scripture hath said, out of his belly shall
flow rivers of living water" (John 7:37,38). Also we see that Jesus,
speaking to the Samaritan woman at the well in Sychar, said, "If thou
knewest the gift of God, and who it is that saith to thee, Give me to
drink; thou wouldest have asked of Him, and He would have given
thee living water" (John 4:10). Then when she challenged Him because He had no bucket or vase to draw the water out of the well,
He told her, "Whosoever drinketh of this water shall thirst again: but
whosoever drinketh of the water that I shall give him shall never
thirst; but the water that I shall give him shall be in him a well of
water springing up into everlasting life" (John 4:13,14).

At first, this might seem a mishmash of ill-used counterweights
and balances with some of the parts missing or the writer's hand on
the scale. But with a good hard look and a good juggling act you will
see that these elements, no matter how seemingly adverse, do really
tie together--and without a slipknot.

But first we have to get back to basics:

1) We believe that He is (or is all He says He is) and that "He is a rewarder of them that diligently seek Him" (Hebrews 11:6).

2) We can come to Him like a Father and, in exchange for our concerns, our burdens, our hurts and bruises, He will give us His peace and rest.

3) As He reveals His lovingkindness and generous nature, we can have the confidence to ask anything in His Name, knowing it is ours (John 14:13; 16:24).

4) We have to understand that asking and receiving and the excitement of a more intimate relationship with Him creates a thirst for more, at which point we come to the living water that is bubbling up through our spirit man.

5) We begin to take of the water of life freely (Revelation 22:17), up to and including overflowing.

6) We can easily satisfy the thirst of others who catch the vision of our springing up into everlasting life and want to join us.

7) Having enthusiastically participated in all His commandments and spread abroad all His precepts with joy and thanksgiving, we have peace like a river--a great river running to the sea.

To conclude this chapter on agreement, I suggest such a prayer as this:

I thank You, Father, that You have shown me the path for my life and that, in all ways, I can agree with You, Your written word (or the logos) and Your Living Word, the Lord Jesus Christ. And I know, Father, that as I come into perfect harmony with Your commandments and precepts, no concern, care, hurt or affliction will have a place in me, because I will fully comprehend the meaning of being one with You. Your word says if I walk in the light, as the Lord Jesus is in the light, we can walk together and have fellow-

ship with one another, where there is only healing, health and wholeness. This I pray in the Name of Jesus.   Amen. and Amen.

9
Healing, Health and Wholeness
By Believing and Receiving from God

If thou canst believe
Read Mark 9:23

Whether or not they are Christian, few people fail to recognize the importance of believing. Jesus said to the father of the epileptic boy, "If thou canst believe, all things are possible to him that believeth." That is so simple and profound, isn't it.

But while great store is set on believing, it has great need for a strong ally--receiving. There are few combinations of complementary words as powerful as *believing* and *receiving*. They make excellent twins: though not identical, they are strong, positive and healthy. And when we can walk before God with them, hand in hand, we will know His approval and absolute victory. No weapon formed against us can prosper--nor can any enemy stand before such a power structure.

However, as in most other good things, there is a "but." But whom do you believe concerning what? And where do you stand with receiving from whom?

As I was learning to walk with the Lord, when anyone admitted to being a believer, I believed him. I knew what I meant by being a believer, and I assumed everybody else had the same definition. Then, as I began to listen more carefully, I was astonished to find there were as many types and descriptions of believers as there were kinds of spaghetti.

There were those who believed in One God, but couldn't believe that Jesus Christ was relevant. There were those who believed
that Jesus was a nice man or a prophet or a magician or a madman--
but couldn't understand how God could subject Him to such a
miserable death. Then there were the ones who believed in the
Trinity--the "three in One," they called Him, like sewing-machine
oil--but couldn't receive the fact that Jesus *is* the Trinity--God the
Father, God the Son and God the Holy Spirit. Further, there were
those who had no problem believing Jesus was the Son of God but
couldn't believe He could save, heal, or perform miracles, because
their church believed all *that* ceased with the death of the apostles.
But the scriptures assure us that Jesus Christ is the same yesterday
and today and for ever (Hebrews 13:8), not just until the apostles
and their influence died out.

Still others believe it is necessary to live on the brink of destitu-
tion in order to serve the God of all glory who promised us abundant
life (John 10:10). And then there are those born-again, Spirit-filled
believers who believe and receive the most outrageous lies from the
devil and then attempt to explain them away in order to protect
God's reputation. Those who are altogether deceived believe that
God somehow uses sickness, poverty and disaster to teach us some-
thing--all the while testifying to His love, goodness and mercy.

As you can see, I have barely scratched the surface. There are
many people who call themselves believers--including the recklessly
tolerant type who lump Buddha, Krishna, Mohammed, Judaism, the
Football Hall of Fame and Christianity all together into one massive
indigestible stew. They are the sliding-board waxers, the contemporary Laodiceans, whom God is going to spew out of His mouth
(Revelation 3:14-16).

But there are also some genuine Christians--born-again, Spirit-
filled people who take God at His Word, know Jesus Christ as Lord
and Savior, believe God's promises and joyously receive every
bounty. They are the happiest and most fulfilled people on earth.
Are you one of them, embracing God's unalterable promises, believ-

ing all He says and receiving His exceeding great reward (Genesis 15:1) which includes strength, health, peace, vigor, joy, youth, the love of God and life in Christ Jesus, our Lord? All of these things belong to us in addition to riches and honor, houses and lands and a closer walk with the God of all glory and everlasting life. If you want anything beyond these things, you're just going to have to pray better, longer and more consistently.

What things soever ye desire
Mark 11:24

"What things soever ye desire, when ye pray, believe that ye receive them, and ye shall have them." When are you to believe and receive? At the very moment you pray. At first glance this might seem outrageous. But this is precisely what Jesus said. And when you catch the principle involved and grasp the long-term benefits, you will fairly leap for joy.

This is a part of the seedtime-and-harvest principle. When the farmer plants corn, he can't see it, hear it, taste it, touch it or smell it. The day after he plants it, he is neither surprised nor indignant that the full corn in the ear is not standing there waiting for the sickle. Nor at the time of harvest is he filled with wonder and amazement (as the Bible says) that there is a great field of corn instead of lima beans or turnips.

Whether or not he knows the scriptures or is a praying man, he quite possibly begins his year with a positive confession. Normally he wouldn't say, "I planted some seeds," but would say, "I planted my crop," which implies the expectation of a harvest that will belong to him. Then, regardless of his spiritual condition, he demonstrates another God-ordained law: "So is the kingdom of God, as if a man should cast seed into the ground; and should sleep, and rise night and day, and the seed should spring and grow up, he knoweth not how. For the earth bringeth forth fruit of herself; first the blade, then the ear, after that the full corn in the ear" (Mark 4:26-28). Can you see how that relates to Mark 11:24?

As long as this farmer's actions--from plowing to planting to harvest--stay within the boundaries of God's immutable laws, he will have a crop. I know, because I never fail to have a crop when I scrupulously follow the laws of sowing and reaping and believing and receiving. In fact, such a crop failure is as impossible as living without breathing. However, most of us are guilty of using human logic to override the laws of God, thus permitting the evil one to put the ring in your nose and guide you into all uncertainty. That is his role and he plays his part with great (if misguided) artistry.

For those who put no stock in the reality of the evil one, that old serpent, which is the devil and Satan (according to Revelation 20:2), who regard him as a figment of man's imagination, I say to you, "At the appointed time, he is going to kill you, whether you know him or not." Oh, he will not come with a sword, or a bottle of poison, or in some very obvious way. He is subtle. As the Word says, "Now the serpent was more subtil than any beast of the field which the Lord God made" (Genesis 3:1). Though contemporary English spells *subtle* differently, there is no mistaking the meaning: he was and is the deceiver. He is going to come at you with deception, as he did Eve. He is going to cause you to challenge God's promises--because he is going to attack you through the thoughts and intents of your heart (Hebrews 4:12), that area in which God wishes to be your guide. If he can get you off balance, get your eyes focused on yourself and your problem, your feelings and emotions, he will defeat you as he did Eve (and then Adam, of course).

But while we are right here, I would like to get Adam and Eve off the hook, as the expression goes. I have heard them blasphemed and maligned, cursed and blamed for the fall of man. And several big ministries have used the indictment that they committed high treason--the implication being that they did this against God. For years these things have bothered me. Not so much the curses and indictment as the fact that Eve, the helpmeet of the most brilliant man in all history (with the exception of Jesus), could be deceived by a snake. What with all the magnificent, as well as funny, animals that were created, how could she have been deceived by the most loath-some one? Then recently I reread the February 1984 issue of a most enlightening publication, *Faith in Action*, in which author R. G. Hardy pointed out:

> If you know what a homograph is, you know that it is a word that has two different meanings although both are spelled the same, such as *pine*, "to languish," and *pine*, "a tree." Likewise is the Hebrew word for serpent, *nachash*, and it means "shining one, beguiler and enchanter." Because the snake is an enchant-er, the interpreters used the word *snake* here instead of its other meaning, "shining one." Do you believe that Eve would have talked to an ole snake? No, Satan came into the garden as a glorious creature. Our English version says that he was wiser than all of the beasts of the earth, but it does not mean "wild animal." This is the same word that is translated *beast* in Revela-tion and it means "a living creature." This *nachash* was wiser than any living creature that God created. He came into the gar-den upright and beautiful. He had beautiful wings and he was a glorious creature. That was ole Lucifer, the shining one, that was ole Satan, the devil, the anointed cherub.

The paragraph above is merely an excerpt: but the entire article is well worth reading. Not nearly enough people know about Satan and his influence in the lives of man.

The things you desire are always at hand and available--or God wouldn't have had His Spirit inspire Mark 11:24. So if your desire is for healing, health and wholeness, what is holding you back? Have you prayed and believed and received? Do you believe that God heals but are in doubt as to whether He has healed or will heal you? Are you double-minded about the whole healing process? Do the desires of your heart battle with your flesh (your feelings and emotions)? If any of these questions have witnessed to your inner man, perhaps you should consider this prayer:

Heavenly Father--Lord of all glory--search my heart--that I may know how to overcome any and all doubts, any and all unbelief, any and all adverse wondering. My mind is constantly being bombarded by negative thoughts and intents that my heart should override. But Father, I must admit to failing too often. I have presented my body a living sacrifice, according to your Word (Romans 12:1), to the extent of my understanding. And further, I have done everything I know to do about believing and receiving. So I ask You, Father, by Your Spirit in my inner man, to teach me in those areas where I lack understanding and to give me those scriptures that will edify and lift me up. And Father, I know I need teaching on the wonders of intercession, so that as I use Your Word for the benefit of other people and other nations, I will have a closer walk with You, which is the ultimate goal, eh, Father? Now Father, I speak the Word of faith, following Your pattern, in calling those things that be not as though they are: I confess that I am healed, healthy and whole because I have overcome Satan by the blood of the Lamb, and the word of my testimony, which I say is unshakable, by the Name of the Lamb, the living Lord Jesus Christ of Nazareth, who is the same yesterday and today and forever.   *Amen--and Amen*

Believe ye that I am able to do this?
Read Matthew 9:27-31

"Believe ye that I am able to do this?" If you are asking the Lord for healing and/or restoration and He asked you that question--as He did the two blind men--would your answer be, "Yea, Lord"? Would you have to stop and think? Or would your answer be couched in words like, "Just as soon as I feel sure I will let you know"? If you are in unbelief, only His grace, goodness and mercy can overshadow your doubts. Otherwise, He would be violating His own Word, which I have seen Him do only on very few occasions.

You do understand that God's wanting you in agreement with His Word is in your own best interest. As you believe the things He has promised and receive them as your own, He is most able to fulfill them.

The Word says, "Is My hand shortened at all, that it cannot redeem? or have I no power to deliver? ... Behold, the Lord's hand is not shortened, that it cannot save; neither his ear heavy, that it cannot hear: but your iniquities have separated between you and your God, and your sins have hid His face from you, that He will not hear" (Isaiah 50:2b; 59:1,2 author's paraphrase).

What He is asking you, beloved, is this: "Do you truly believe that He has bought you back from the storehouse of the evil one? Or do you think that He is somehow incapable of delivering you from your distresses?" He is also asking if you will or won't consider Him able to save you from everlasting death and separation from Him. Is the reason somehow involved with your iniquities and sins, especially those He has forgotten and has put as far from you as the east is from the west? Is your undoing self-condemnation, which is the same as iniquity and sin because it is based on pride, which causes you to completely focus on self? Are you so self-oriented, self-centered and, therefore, self-deluded that you can't see the grass for the field, the trees for the forest, His love for His blessings?

If you are saved and filled with the Holy Spirit, the Word says of you, "There is therefore now no condemnation to them which are in Christ Jesus, who walk not after the flesh, but after the Spirit" (Romans 8:1). Any self-condemnation is sin. You are saying, in effect, that the Word of God is somehow either misquoted or wrong. But that simply cannot be, for the writer of Hebrews tells us, "He [Jesus] is able to save them [you] to the uttermost that come unto God by Him, seeing He ever liveth to make intercession for them [you]" (Hebrews 7:25). Where it says, "save to the uttermost"--which, in the Greek, is *panteles*, meaning "save completely, entirely and forever"--could this in any way exclude healing, health and wholeness? Of course not. God is neither cruel or unfeeling. However, it is incumbent upon us to understand that God has a pre-established program. Otherwise it couldn't possibly fit all needs for all men for all time. It would have to change from second to second to accommodate every momentary transaction. When we will to fit into His plan, we find every need for all men for all time has been foreseen from the foundation of the world--and His perfect provision is standing there staring us in the face.

Beloved, I urge you to address those earlier questions. What is it you believe? Where are you with regard to what God says about you specifically? One of the areas where we are most likely to give ground to the devil is as he attacks us through our personal thoughts, feelings and emotions--thereby setting a place for himself at our spiritual table. The Word exhorts us to give him no place (Ephesians 4:27). Some Christian wag has said, "Never invite the devil to dinner because he will invariably bring his toothbrush and pajamas in preparation for an extended stay."

The reason I keep coming back to those questions is that the Lord has shown me that Christians can see miracle after miracle and never relate them to their own situation. Instead of confessing, "If God will do it for them, He will do it for me," they tend to attribute some special personal condition to the miraculous. Like, "Sure God can do it for him/her--he/she is tall, short, fat, thin, an executive, a bum, a minister, a sinner, whatever." But God is no respecter of persons; the Bible tells us that over and over again. You have to see yourself as valuable and precious in the sight of God, not as some spiritual castaway or derelict. For when you have settled this in your inner man and know and understand it in the depth of your being, you can believe and receive all He has for you. And nothing can by any means hurt or destroy you because "He shall cover thee with His feathers, and under His wings shalt thou trust: His truth shall be thy shield and buckler. Thou shalt not be afraid for the terror by night; nor for the arrow that flieth by day; nor for the pestilence that walketh in darkness; nor for the destruction that wasteth at noonday" (Psalm 91:4-6).

This is the work of God
Read John 6:24-29

"This is the work of God," Jesus said, "that ye believe on Him whom He hath sent." The truth is, we greatly resemble the people He was addressing. He had walked on the water to His disciples' boat in the dark. The multitude hadn't seen Him leave the mountain where He fed the five thousand. So when they missed Him and His disciples, "they also took shipping, and came to Capernaum, seeking for Jesus. And when they had found Him on the other side of the sea, they said unto Him, Rabbi, when camest Thou hither?" (John 6:24,25).

After rebuking them for failure to see the miracles and accusing them of following Him merely for the sake of the food He had supplied, He tells them, "Labour not for the meat which perisheth, but for that meat which endureth unto everlasting life, which the Son of man shall give unto you: for Him hath God the Father sealed" (John 6:27).

Then they asked the most ridiculous question in all of recorded history. After asking Him what they might do to do the works of God, and Jesus answering, "Believe on Him whom God has sent," they asked, "What sign shewest Thou?"

Can you imagine? Just the afternoon before, He had fed five thousand men besides women and children (Matthew 14:21) with five barley loaves and two small fishes, and here they are asking for a sign. Could anything be more outrageous? Hardly.

But isn't that just like us? Don't we daily see the miracles of God? Day following night; the sun, the moon, the stars; the simple flexing of our fingers; the steam of our breath on a frosty morning; the character of nature reflected in the seasons; man, beast, flowers and trees producing after their kind? And aren't some of us still guilty of asking dumb questions: "So why doesn't He just go ahead and heal me?"

Yeah, Lord, what sign shewest Thou? Show me something I can believe.

If you ever ask any of these questions and you hear a voice within, saying, "Like what?" I urge you to kneel, repent and ask His forgiveness so, in your ignorance, the devil doesn't crush you like a bug. Because, under such circumstances, He would certainly have the authority.

But if you do what Jesus said, i.e., believe on the Lord Jesus Christ, God will intervene in all of your affairs because you are working the works of God. When you do this, beloved, with all your heart (spirit or inner man), you have an unbreakable covenant with the living God and all of His promises become yours, every last one.

Repent ye, and believe the gospel
Read Mark 1:13-15

After being "there in the wilderness forty days, tempted of Satan . . . Jesus came into Galilee, preaching the gospel of the kingdom of God, and saying, The time is fulfilled, and the kingdom of God is at hand: repent ye, and believe the gospel" (Mark 1:13-15). Did Jesus say, "Repent ye, and believe" because, without having repented, it is difficult to believe? I don't know about you--or Bible scholars for that matter--but I believe that repentance is so tied to forgiveness and forgiveness is so intertwined with the love in Him that repentance is one of God's primary requirements.

In my own case, a number of weeks passed before I knew anything about repentance. And it wasn't until I had a heart understanding of the necessity for it that I really got before God in reconciliation and restoration. No one actually led me to the Lord. It was my habit to lie in my gigantic tub each morning from seven to eight and read some book or other. And it was after an evening at church, where there was a healing service, that, while reading, I began to weep and cry out to God. "O God," I kept saying, "I'm a sinner. O God, I'm a sinner."

Although this shouldn't have been a revelation to me, I assure you it was. I had committed almost every "thou shalt not"--short of rape and murder--and I was of the school of thought that since all my friends did it, it must be all right. Ridiculous? Yes, but true. That was the way it was. Though I was sorry in my heart for all my sinful enterprises, there was no one to tell me about repentance.

A number of weeks later, I read Dr. Derek Prince's book on scriptural repentance, called, strangely enough, *Repent and Believe*. I knew immediately what I had to do and went about doing it. What a revelation! What astonishing results! How simple and practical are God's ways. Enter forgiveness and the love of God in Christ Jesus the Lord. It was done.

For you who have little knowledge of sin and its implications, the following facts will greatly help you to healing, health and wholeness. In the first place, all sin is sin; there is no such thing as little sins and big sins. The man with the palsy, the woman taken in the very act of adultery and the woman who was quite possibly a prostitute had this in common: they were all instantly forgiven by the Lord Jesus. In none of these accounts does it say they were repentant or that they even asked for forgiveness.

And although Jesus took the sins of the entire world on Himself--past, present and future--He had not yet gone to the cross where all sin was to be dealt with forever. But the Bible tells us, "God commendeth His love toward us, in that, while we were yet sinners, Christ died for us" (Romans 5:8). And again, "He [God] hath made him [Jesus] to be sin for us, who knew no sin; that we might be made the righteousness of God in Him" (2 Corinthians 5:21). We can see by these scriptures that God was forecasting His forgiveness for all men in much the same way as He did day and night and time and seasons.

It is all important that you understand this: your sins have already been paid for to the uttermost. Whether you are a sinner or a saint, every last vestige of sin in your life has been purchased by the blood of Jesus on the cross. It has been totally wiped away.

Therefore, beloved, if you are a Spirit-filled believer and are plagued by a consciousness of sin, you are quite possibly in gross error. If Jesus has already paid the supreme penalty for all sin--past,

present and future (I reiterate for emphasis)--you could be up to
your armpits in pride. You quite possibly have your concerns so centered in self that you are missing the most spectacular blessing in all
Christendom--total freedom and purity in the sight of God Almighty,
who alone could devise anything so outrageous and then see to
making it a matter of truth.

If such is the case, you ought to seriously consider this prayer:

*Wonderful Father, glorious Lord, this day I enter Your gates with
thanksgiving and come into Your courts with praise. I worship
You with a song of love in my heart. I exalt the Name of Jesus, as
I kneel here before You, heavenly Father. It is possible I have
been in error, believing that I was somehow acting in an attitude
of humility, when, in reality, I was thinking more of myself than I
should, which has been pointed out to me as pride. Since Your
Word clearly shows You detest this form of self-centered pride, I
repent of every action to do with pride and I ask Your forgiveness.
Also, Father, I renounce all manner of self-interest, self-esteem,
self-satisfaction and self-love that is not instituted by You.*

*Every lying spirit and every deceiving spirit, I speak to you in
the Name of Jesus and put you on notice that I will never again
entertain any false images of self. I tell you, you are bound. By the
power of God and in the Name of Jesus, I rebuke you and command you to flee. Now, Holy Father, I thank You and praise You
for Your Spirit that dwells in me--and I set my face like a flint to
be more and more open--so I can be guided and led into all truth,
as I take You by the hand by faith. All this, Father, I commit to
Your care, in the Name of Jesus.*   *Amen--and Amen*

He that believeth on Me
Read John 6:47

"He that believeth on Me hath everlasting life," Jesus said. But many
of us live in error because we take this to mean that we have everlasting life only after we die. The Bible says, "He that believeth on the

Son of God hath the witness in himself: he that believeth not God hath made Him [God] a liar; because he believeth not the record that God gave of His Son. And this is the record, that God hath given [past tense] to us eternal life, and this life is in His Son. He that hath the son hath life; and he that hath not the Son of God hath not life" (1 John 5:10-12).

Which are you? A believer or a believe-notter? Jesus clearly made healing, health, wholeness and every other good thing so simple that it is astonishing that we don't grasp the truth of it immediately. Its very simplicity becomes a snare: for we say, "If it is all that simple, why doesn't He--?" What we need to say is, "Since He has given me the power of choice, and it is so simple, I will--"

We have to *will* to do those things He has clearly given us His authority to do--heal the sick, cleanse the lepers, raise the dead (including ourselves, of course)--for He said, "Freely ye have received, freely give" (Matthew 10:8). If He has freely given us His authority and we have received it, are we freely giving? Giving and receiving is one of the many God principles and it carries through every area of our lives. If we give money, we receive goods, services or blessings; if we give seed, we receive crops, fruits or blessings; and if we give goods, services or blessings, we receive monetary gain or other tangible returns or blessings. With all laws--God's and man's-- there is a positive recompense of reward. Jesus said, "Give, and it shall be given unto you; good measure, pressed down, and shaken together, and running over, shall men give into your bosom. For with the same measure that ye mete withal it shall be measured to you again" (Luke 6:38).

Many pastors and teachers quote this scripture as an incentive for tithing, but I believe it has little to do with money. If I understand what the Bible teaches about tithing, if I give a tenth (the tithe) of what I receive--whether goods, services, money or love--depending on what I am believing for, I can receive a thirty, sixty or a hundred-fold return. But this scripture really only promises that if I give I will receive a good, solid return--not thirty, sixty or a hundred fold. It says that with what measure I give, that is the measure I will be given.

We have often heard it quoted: "God so loved that He gave." Of course, we know this means that God gave us Jesus Christ. But do we realize that He gave Jesus so that He might receive us--you and me? Regardless of how we feel about the transaction--God's giving Jesus for us--God apparently thought it was a good deal. Would He have considered it otherwise?

With this question ringing in our thoughts, let's get back to "He that believeth on Me hath everlasting life." Jesus is not talking about everlasting life beginning with your death; He is talking about everlasting life beginning when you believe on Him and that God sent Him for you and me. At that point your heart knows the whole truth: that He was sent for you; that by believing and receiving Him you will also receive all that He has for you, not the least of which is healing, health and wholeness in spirit, soul and body.

The Word doesn't say that He came to give you sickness and that more abundantly but He came to give you life and that more abundantly. Life is certainly not considered abundant in the midst of afflictions. That would be a travesty, if Jesus were responsible for such nonsense. But He isn't. He is the author of life, its perpetuator --even its finisher, not as it relates to death but as it relates to quality of life. In the same sense that He is the author and finisher of our faith (Hebrews 12:2), He is the author and finisher of our lives. In fact, without Jesus as central to all we believe, do and think, we become like most of today's containers: throwaways. Do you see that, beloved? *What kind of container are you? What do you contain? In what capacity? And for how long?*

The Bible exhorts us to be filled with the Spirit (Ephesians 5:18b), which is the Holy Spirit of God. That is the only way we can successfully get our eyes off our problems, our pains, our sufferings, our afflictions, our sicknesses, our . . . our . . . our . . . Because, when we are filled with Him (not *it*), our joy is full.

When we become totally self-centered--having our thoughts centered in our feelings and emotions--we don't have any understanding of where we are. Then, instead of believing and receiving from God, who assures us that He is the Lord that healeth us, we believe and receive from the evil one, who tells us our problems and sorrows are from God, and we don't know the difference. What a shameful situation.

But I have this glorious news: the Bible is true from cover to cover. And you are the only one who can make it of none effect--by not believing and not receiving. If you are ill and truly want to be well and whole, Jesus said, "What things soever ye desire, when ye pray, believe that ye receive them, and ye shall have them" (Mark 11:24).

A part of the simplest of your daily prayers can, therefore, be:

I thank You, Father, that, since Your Word instructs me to do so, in the matter of my complete and total healing, I believe I receive.

Amen--and Amen

10
Healing, Health and Wholeness
Through the Power of Prayer

After this manner therefore pray ye
Read Matthew 6:8-13

"After this manner therefore pray ye . . . " Having so said, Jesus went on to teach His disciples what has come to be known as "The Lord's Prayer." And what a prayer it is! It covers nearly every area of man's need. It begins with praise and worship; it has supplication for our needs and the needs of others; it encompasses forgiveness for all; it asks for guidance and protection from the evil (one); and it ends with the affirmation of our beliefs, that God is the possessor of heaven and earth, for which we praise and worship Him. That is a lot of information to get into four little sentences, isn't it?

But God isn't impressed with long prayers, especially those of the haranguing and pleading variety. If, as Jesus assures us, "Your Father knoweth what things ye have need of, before ye ask Him," what purpose could be served by long and agonizing prayers? This is not to say you should only be brief or calculatedly succinct--for the Lord loves your fellowship with Him whether in long or short prayers--but our greatest need in the prayer department is to know what we should pray for as we ought (Romans 8:26,27).

Most people I have asked--where they were open enough to discuss how they pray--admit that their prayers are either vague or nebulous and that they are not satisfied with them or confident that they will be answered. But after a brief teaching on the specifics of prayer, they come to understand that God's fondest desire is to do wonderful things for His children and they greatly rejoice at the acceleration of their answers. Of course, the reason they are getting more answers is that they are praying for specific things that God can unhesitatingly give.

Unfortunately, too many prayers go something like this: "Now, God, You know I need transportation." And the devil, who also hears, sends them a rusty bicycle, and they say, "Praise the Lord!" if somewhat half-heartedly. And they will possibly never know the disappointment in the heart of God for their lack of discernment. If they could hear the voice of God, they would hear Him say, "*I don't have* any rusty bicycles."

God wants you to be aware that "every good gift and every perfect gift is from above, and cometh down from the Father of lights, with whom is no variableness, neither shadow of turning" (James 1:17). He wants you to realize His unalterably perfect nature, a nature that finds fulfillment only in giving, which can be hampered by our undefined desires or goals. So if you want a purple ten-speed bicycle with a blue leather seat and chrome wheels, handle bars and carrier, *say so.* Then, when it comes, you won't have to wonder who sent it, and even more importantly, why. God sent it because you asked Him. And there is something else you might want to consider: you might give Him the option of improving the specifications for His own pleasure.

Most of us think of prayer as the means whereby we can receive something from God, which is certainly one of its purposes. But there are many kinds of prayer and each has many elements and facets. When we ask for something, that is a prayer of supplication, which the Bible suggests we link with thanksgiving (Philippians 4:6). There are also prayers of dedication, consecration, intercession, affirmation, commemoration, confession (which the Bible calls *profession*)--I could go on and on. Within each of these categories there can be broad elements of such diversity as to exhaust the soul-- people, places and things; drought, floods, disasters; sickness, sorrow and death; you name it. That is the reason we should keep our prayers simple and concise; it is far easier to exercise our faith on one specific thing than it is to grasp hold of all the complexities of a world society.

We need to know our limitations and the extent of our faith, so we can have a broad plateau from which to launch our ascent. Then we can steadfastly move onward and upward to ever-increasing achievements.

Where we wish to have the most successful prayer life, we must at least ponder the prayers of Jesus Christ as our example. His prayers were simple and direct, not spattered with hosts of off-setting possibilities, not blurred by multitudes of verities. He always got the answer He was seeking--not just *an* answer but *the* answer because of His close walk with the Father and His always being led by the Spirit.

In the matter of prayer for healing, many scholars and teachers would like to place it near the bottom of the list. Such prayers, they say, tend to focus on the problem rather than on the solution and are, therefore, basically negative. But that is like lumping all cancer under the incurable label. There just aren't any hard-and-fast rules with God. He can cure cancer with the same ease as He can cure the adolescent pimple. But as in everything else, He wants to act in con-cert with us so that He is always able to honor His Word, which says (and this is my favorite verse), "Before they call [pray], I will answer; and while they are yet speaking, I will hear" (Isaiah 65:24). When en-tered into by a sealed servant of the living God--willingly yielded, guided and led by the Holy Spirit--nothing is more powerful than a prayer for healing or a prayer for world peace, because God is in the midst.

A good beginning question for you is this one: "Are your prayers guided and led by God's Holy Spirit?" If you don't know the answer to that question, perhaps you should address this one: "Are you filled with the Holy Spirit?" If you can't answer that in the affirm-ative, "Do you assuredly know whether or not you have been born again?" Or, to say it another way, "Have you been born of the Spirit of God?"

If any of these questions are a mystery to you, beloved, or if you are in any way uncertain of the answers, there is a prayer God made the simplest of all. It is called the prayer of salvation, which ideally is followed by the prayer for the infilling of the Holy Spirit. The prayer of salvation goes like this:

> *Dear heavenly Father, I come before You as a sinner and I repent of my sin and turn back to You. Please forgive me for being so long coming to this day. And now I ask You, Jesus Christ, to come into my heart and be my personal Lord and Savior. Now Father, while I have Your ear, I ask You, according to Luke 11:11-13, for Your blessed Holy Spirit--that I be totally filled so that Your great power and might will be able to flow in and through me.*
> *Amen--and Amen*

Could anything be more simple? Of course not. But that is the way God is. He wouldn't just create you as an act of supreme personal love and then make it difficult to get to Him. He is always perfectly and impartially fair; that is His nature and you are His child.

I will pray the Father
Read John 14:16-18

"I will pray the Father," Jesus said, "and He shall give you another Comforter, that He may abide with you for ever; even the Spirit of truth; whom the world cannot receive, because it seeth him not, neither knoweth him: but ye know him; for he dwelleth with you, and shall be in you. I will not leave you comfortless: I will come to you."

When Jesus was on the earth in the form of a man, He was the manifested presence of the Holy Spirit. In other words, He was God the Father, God the Son and God the Holy Spirit--setting forth Their example through an earthly being or body. As He is speaking to His disciples, He says of Himself (as the Holy Spirit), "He dwel-

leth with you, and shall be in you" (John 14:17b). Further along,
Jesus says to them, "But the Comforter, which is the Holy Ghost,
whom the Father will send in My Name, He shall teach you all
things, and bring all things to your remembrance, whatsoever I have
said unto you" (John 14:26).

Here we see one of the manifold ways the Holy Spirit is important to our walk with the Lord. He is the Presence of God who
abides with us forever. He is the Revelator of all truth; when we invoke the Name of Jesus, He is our teacher, our guide, our leader and
the One who brings to our remembrance everything Jesus has taught
us. But this is not nearly the all He truly is--the all in all.

I have heard many people say, "Oh, if only I could have lived in
Jesus' day. Imagine being there, seeing and hearing Him, maybe
even getting to touch Him." But as for me and my house, we prefer
being in the here and now. Why? Because when Jesus walked the
earth as a man, if we had been in Capernaum and He in Nazareth,
we would have been miles apart. Or if He had been in Samaria and
we in Jerusalem, we would still have been miles apart, perhaps even
far enough apart that we wouldn't even have heard of Him. But now,
by His Holy Spirit being within us, no matter where we are in all the
earth, He is with us always, even to the end of the world.

Although being either Peter, James or John might have really
been nifty--for they were with Him much of the time until His death,
burial and resurrection--they had only the tiniest glimmer of what
He was all about.

The importance of that particular truth is this: at the point we
are able to totally yield ourselves to the Spirit of God, we will be able
to know everything Jesus taught, every example He gave and every
tiny detail of His day-to-day life--because the Spirit of life is no
longer out there somewhere, it is within us.

For you who spend much time praying in the Spirit (i.e., in your
heavenly language), it is no revelation to say that it is possible for us
to change the world. Whereas, those do-gooder bleeding hearts who

go about protesting against America's nuclear policy will do little more than confuse the issues with their empty hopes.

It will be the millions yielded to the Spirit who will loose the good and bind the evil, who will loose the bands of wickedness, who will undo the heavy burdens of the oppressed and set them free, who will cut in sunder the yokes of bondage and open the prison gates (Isaiah 58; Psalm 24). How? By their heavenly language, the only language that can utter unalterably perfect prayers that God can use to do great exploits and show forth His mighty hand and stretched-out arm.

As we have written in an earlier chapter, God has set bounds for Himself which He will not violate for any reason. Why? Because He has already bestowed on us all of His authority in heaven and earth (Matthew 28:18-20). Here we see, in effect, the God of the universe putting His dependence on you and me to show Himself mighty. That is outrageous, isn't it? In fact, the Bible says, "This is an hard saying; who can hear it?" (John 6:60). But this shows us one of the most thrilling aspects of prayer--to release to God the full authority to work in and through us.

Following is a prayer that will help you shed some light on this aspect of the dominion we have been given and what to do with it:

I thank You, Father, Lord of heaven and earth, that through the Lord Jesus You have transferred His authority to me. Father, I am not unaware of the awesome responsibility this entails--nor am I any the less human, Father. And I must say it causes me to wonder in my heart at my own worthiness to receive such a charge. But Your Word tells me that I need have no concern-- because I was not made worthy by any higher effort of my own but wholly by worthiness imparted to me by the Lord Jesus. Yes, Father, I see that He became sin that I might be made righteous; He was made poor that I might be made rich; and He took our diseases and infirmities that we might have His health. Father, I know this great transfer could only have been the inspired creativ-

ity of the true and living God. So I worship and praise You,
Abba Father, with stammering lips and another tongue (as
Isaiah says), asking You in the Name of Jesus and by Your pre-
cious Holy Spirit how to use Your mighty gifts entirely for Your
purposes, O God.   *Amen--and Amen*

What wilt thou?
Read Mark 10:46-52

"What wilt thou that I should do unto thee?" Jesus asked blind Bartimaeus as He was leaving Jericho for Bethany. Like so many of us
when we want something from the Lord, Bartimaeus kicked up quite
a fuss, which in itself didn't amount to a hill of beans. You can say,
of course, "Well, he certainly captured the Lord's attention." But,
beloved, if you are a born-again, Spirit-filled believer, you *always*
have the Lord's attention, and you don't have to kick up a fuss to get
it. Besides which, Bartimaeus could have hooted and hollered till a
week from Tuesday and it wouldn't have done him one earthly bit of
good. What it takes is your answer to Jesus' question: "What wilt
thou that I should do unto thee?" In Bartimaeus' case, he answered,
"Lord, that I might receive *my* sight." Notice, beloved, that Bartimaeus was asking only for that which belonged to him by God's
promise.

There is something here that all of us must get firmly established in our hearts: God wants us to have everything that belongs to
us by inheritance and none of the things we inadvertently claim, such
as *my* cold, *my* headache, *my* arthritis, *my* high blood pressure. How
are you going to successfully pray to get rid of something you are calling your own? Do you see what I am saying? It only really belongs to
you when you accept it and call it yours.

As thoughtless as this kind of confession is, God will still
joyously give you what is rightfully yours--but I have never seen Him
take away anything that people claim to be theirs.

You can see by this it is all important to guard our words. We
can say, "I have a headache," the same way we might say, "I have a

dollar." And both can be gotten rid of with relative ease. But the moment they become *my* headache and *my* dollar, they tend to cling like polyester and you need some spiritual static remover. Bible teacher (and rice farmer) Charles Capps, in his little pamphlet, "God's Creative Power," tells about teaching from this text when the Lord spoke up and said, "I have told My people they can *have what they say*, and they are *saying what they have*."

When we attempt to fight some sickness or affliction with prayer, it is necessary we begin by understanding this premise: God has already given us every weapon needed for our total victory--even triumph. But to see the victory, we are going to have to use the weapons God has given us: *the words of our mouths*. The Bible tells us, "Though we walk in the flesh, we do not war after the flesh: (For the weapons of our warfare are not carnal, but mighty through God to the pulling down of strong holds;) casting down imaginations, and every high thing that exalteth itself against the knowledge of God, and bringing into captivity every thought to the obedience of Christ; and having in a readiness to revenge all disobedience, when your obedience is fulfilled" (2 Corinthians 10:3-6).

A closer study of the weapons of our warfare and our protective armor is revealing: we are to have our loins girt about with truth, having on the breastplate of righteousness, our feet shod with the preparation of the gospel of peace, taking the shield of faith against the fiery darts of the evil one, wearing the helmet of salvation and having the sword of the Spirit, which is *the Word of God* (see Ephesians 6:14-17).

Do you know that His armor and the weapons of our warfare already belong to us as part of the many gifts of God? Whether you realize it or not, they do. But all too many of us are trying to fight our spiritual battle with earthly weapons, which the Word calls worldly, fleshly or carnal. Simple logic tells us the devil would have been done in long ago if he could be stabbed, shot or strangled. But he can't. The big question is: Do we know how to use our spiritual weapons to subdue and defeat him? The truth of God says it is a piece of cake: just use His Word.

The reason the Word tells us not to war after the flesh (i.e., with earthly weapons) is that we are fighting the invisible forces of darkness. We are tearing down strongholds we cannot see with our physical eyes. And we are to cast down vain imaginations that try to plague us through our mental processes, as well as to crush every negative thought that sets itself above the knowledge of God.

For you who are uncertain about how to do these things, the following explanations might be helpful:

1. Strongholds are mostly elements, habit patterns or verbal confessions out of our pasts, things that are continually causing us to stumble for lack of understanding of their power over us. Usually we continue to stumble because we don't truly understand who we are in Christ. Although the Bible assures us we are *a new creation* in Christ, we continue to say things like, "Well, it runs in the family, you know" or "This comes on me every year about this time" or "Just as sure as we get to the beach, we have a week of rain. . . . " You get the picture. But do you realize what you are doing when you confess such things? You are using God's principles in reverse. You are "calling those things that be not [in truth] as though they were," which God did when He said, "Let there be light." As light came, so will your continued afflictions. How? By your *words*.

   The truth is, when you became a new creature (better translated as *creation*) in Christ, old things were to pass away and all things were to become new (2 Corinthians 5:17)--but by bringing these negative thoughts and confessions into the kingdom with you can you make your new creation of none effect. But there is something wonderful to know: although the negative confessions are called *strongholds*, they are easily demolished by your wielding the sword of the Spirit, which is the Word of God--our spiritual bulldozer.

2. Casting down imaginations (vain or otherwise) works in much the
   same way with the sword of the Spirit, the Word of God. As in
   all battles, it is essential to know who our enemy is and what
   weapons he is using. We tend to think of imaginations as things
   allied to dreams or visions. But the imaginations that are set up
   by the evil one to destroy us are different. They are the
   thoughts that come to us from without--for the devil has no
   more place in us than he had in Jesus. When we have a pain or
   a twinge, because of the fear of cancer in the world today we
   begin to wonder: *What is that?* Then the evil one whispers,
   "Could it be--you know--the big 'C'?" Or perhaps you have a
   stiffness in one of your joints and this thought comes to you:
   *Don't discount heredity. You know your mother had arthritis all
   her life.* I won't belabor this line of thought: you get the idea.

      You can see how such thought patterns exalt themselves
   against the knowledge of God, which is His Word. He says, "I
   am the Lord that healeth thee" or "I am the Lord your health"
   (Exodus 15:26). If God the Lord is your health, beloved, and
   the devil is attempting to be your sickness, you have come to
   that valley of decision: you must use the Word of God. Having
   on all the armor of God and the sword of the Lord in your
   mouth, you can boldly say to Satan, "I refuse to receive anything
   from you, you foul thing. Jesus Himself took my infirmities and
   bore my sicknesses [Matthew 8:17; Isaiah 53:3-5], so there is no
   point in both of us carrying them."

      And then you can pray,

> *Lord God, I thank You for Your Word that tells me that
> Jesus is not only my health but my strength, peace, vigor,
> joy, youth, love and life.*   *Amen--and Amen*

3. Allied to the above is this truth: we absolutely must learn to immediately take our thoughts captive and to put them in the
   place of obedience to Christ. Oh, how important that is to un-

derstand! For our human tendency is to mull things over--to ponder, contemplate, muse or ruminate (as a cow chews its cud). This is great when it comes to meditating scriptures, but entertaining thoughts that are harmful is one of the biggies in the no-no department. All you have to do is pick at a blemish and, if Satan isn't sleeping, the first thought that will come to you is, *That's how skin cancer starts, you know.* Then, if he can keep you picking at it and thinking about it, barring divine intervention you will see the manifestation. If you want to know how I know, I will tell you. I did it--and I got it--but thank God I knew the Word that would get it off me and place it under Jesus' administration. I commanded the spot to dry up from the root--and it did. It had to obey.

But first, I had to take all the thoughts about it captive and put them under the Word. Then I had to be constantly aware that I couldn't pick at it. Finally, as I knew in my heart that it could no longer prevail, I also knew the battle was won and that I was victorious in Him. After all, cancer is only a name until you give it dominion through fear; then that fear brings in death. But the Word says that God gave Jesus "a Name that is above every name: that at the Name of Jesus every knee should bow, of things in heaven, and things in earth, and things under the earth; and that every tongue should confess that Jesus Christ is Lord, to the glory of God the Father" (Philippians 2:9-11). And certainly cancer, multiple sclerosis, arthritis, leukemia, pneumonia, heart trouble, allergies, bronchitis, blood pressure, and the like are nothing more than names--*which must bow to the Name of Jesus Christ.*

4. The obedience factor is summed up in two words: *Do it.* Don't just think about it, *do it.* Don't just sit there and wonder about it, *do it.* Unused armor and swords rust; the unused Word of God is equally useless. Throughout the world there are Bibles sitting on shelves, gathering dust, while their owners are carted off to

their graves before their times. So we see the unused Word doesn't do anything, while the Word used with power, especially in obedience, is world-changing, sickness-destroying, Satan-crushing.

The Word says, "The prayer of faith shall save the sick, and the Lord shall raise him up; and if he have committed sins, they shall be forgiven him. Confess your faults one to another, and pray one for another, that ye may be healed. The effectual fervent prayer of a righteous man availeth much" (James 5:15,16).

Right here we are going to have a prayer of faith, the remission of sins, a confession of our faults, a prayer for the healing of others and ourselves. It will be an effectual fervent prayer and it is going to avail much.

Holy Father, I come before You in prayer and supplications with thanksgiving, in the Name of Jesus, confessing what Your Word says about me: that I have overcome the world, the flesh and the devil by the blood of the Lamb and the word of my testimony. I know all the power and authority it took to open the Red Sea is resident in me; and all the power it took to cleanse the leper is resident in me; and all the power that raised Jesus from the dead is resident in me. What a glorious and generous Father You are! And Father, Your Word says You sent that Word to heal me, that He is the Sun of righteousness with healing in His wings, who took my infirmities and bore my sickness, by whose Spirit He is still going about doing good and healing all who are oppressed by the devil and by whose stripes I was and am healed.

Now, Holy Father, according to your Word and in obedience to Christ, I remit the sin of every human being and loose them to hear and understand Your Gospel. And, yes, my Lord and my God, though I am not without many faults and transgressions, I thank You that as You look through the veil of the blood of Jesus, You see me righteous and clean. Oh, what a Lord! Oh, what a Savior! Finally, Father, as I kneel here before You, I, by faith, place every person with any sickness, disease, affliction, pain or suffering on Your altar, where nothing evil can stand. And I believe Your Word that says, "I am the Lord that healeth thee," and I praise and worship and adore You, Father, in the Name of Jesus Christ of Nazareth.   *Amen—and Amen*

11
Healing, Health and Wholeness
By the Power in the Name of Jesus

And these signs shall follow
Read Mark 16:17,18

"And these signs shall follow them that believe in My Name," Jesus said. "They shall cast out devils; they shall speak with new tongues; they shall take up serpents; and if they drink any deadly thing, it shall not hurt them; they shall lay hands on the sick, and they shall recover." You who are meticulous students may have already seen the revelation in these verses. For you who are not, I will let you in on the secret: it is in the punctuation.

There are no punctuation marks in the Hebrew or the Greek, just as there are no chapters and verses, numbered (or otherwise). Yet in the fourteen English-language translations I have checked, there is either a colon, a semicolon or a period after the word *believe*. The King James Version, which I use, says, "And these signs shall follow them that believe; in My Name shall they . . . " And all the other translations I have consulted are punctuated something like that. But the original text reads, "And these signs shall follow them that believe in My Name . . . " It then goes on to say, *"They shall . . . "* It doesn't say anything more about believing in Jesus; He was standing right there in front of them. What He wanted them to understand was that He had given them His Name--just as though He had written them a power of attorney. As a matter of fact, that is what He was doing, giving them His verbal power of attorney, the all-inclusive right to use His Name, and He has given it to us as well.

John confirms this with these words: "He came unto His own, and His own received Him not. But as many as received Him, to them gave He power to become the sons of God, even to them that *believe on His Name*: which were born, not of blood, nor of the will of the flesh, nor of the will of man, but of God" (John 1:11-13). So you can see, beloved, the importance not only of believing in Jesus but believing on His Name. In fact, learning to use His Name may be the most important thing you will learn from this book.

What does the Name of Jesus mean to you personally? Does it speak to you of the power and authority in you, a power and authority so great as to be unshakable or immovable, the power and authority to heal the sick, cleanse the leper, raise the dead, cast out demons? If you have doubts about this power and authority in your life, chances are you have never truly placed yourself in Him or seated yourself in heavenly places with Him.

For most of us when we were little children, there was no more secure place in all the world than Daddy's (or Mother's) lap. When you were there, enfolded in their arms, nothing could by any means harm you. As a consequence, you enjoyed perfect peace and rest for your souls. When your earthly parents can no longer hold you in this way, either because you are too big or they too frail, God has that place of security ready and waiting for you. Though you may not as clearly feel His embrace, what does that prove? When you fell asleep in Daddy's lap, you were not aware when he took you up and tucked you in bed. But because you didn't feel it at the time, it wasn't any less real or true.

When I outgrew my filial lap-sitting, I would climb a tree and look out over the entire world--in my imagination, of course. Or I would sit for hours by a nearby stream, fascinated by the water; or I would go to the pond and watch the tadpoles as they struggled through their metamorphosis from water-breathing amphibians to air-breathing, goggle-eyed frogs. I had no concept, at the time, that God was there with me--enjoying my peace and my rest--listening to the quiet concert of the bees, the dragonflies and the skittering water bugs. But He was there all right, just as He is with you wherever you are this moment and in whatever condition. It is essential, beloved, that you know this, understand it and acknowledge it. Until I was sixty-seven years old, I didn't know that He had been present with me when I was in the tree, or by the stream or the pond. Oh, how many opportunities I missed to talk with Him about His world of love and ponder His plan for my life--which didn't include sickness, pain or suffering and certainly never an untimely death.

God was with my mother the day I brought a snake home in a can and put it under the stove. In those days, stoves stood up on legs, and I didn't put the snake there as an act of mischief: it just seemed like a good, safe place to keep the snake. But my mother saw the can and reached under the stove and picked it up, unfortunately tilting it as she did, and the snake fell out on the floor. Well, you could have heard her screams in Pittsburgh (we lived in Washington, D.C.). I came running and found her standing on a kitchen chair, shrieking at the top of her voice and pointing to the harmless little ten-inch garter snake cringing in the corner. I went over and picked it up and put it back in the can, completely innocent of any wrongdoing. I had just recently graduated from the lap-sitting stage, and I didn't yet know anything about girls and snakes and mice.

Are you wondering what this has to do with your relationship to God and how to use the Name of Jesus in your day-to-day life? Beloved, you need to learn to visualize being in the loving embrace of your heavenly Father, having your confidence, peace and rest centered in Him. For "in Him, we live and move and have our being" (Acts 17:28). Or putting it another way, He is the cause, the sustaining power and the very spirit of our lives. That is a law of God just as gravity is a law. You don't have one shred of doubt when you let go of an object that it is going to fall. It is just as necessary to know with certainty your relationship to God the Lord and Jesus Christ, His Son. As Paul wrote, "For the law of the Spirit of life in Christ Jesus hath made me free from the law of sin and death" (Romans 8:2).

This tells us that there is a law of the Spirit of life and it also shows its adversary, the law of sin and death.

If then there are two such laws, we have to determine which of the two we wish to live under: the law of the Spirit of life in Christ Jesus or the law of sin and death. There certainly shouldn't be any contest there, eh?

In seeking to have understanding of this in your inner man, you might wish to pray a prayer something like the following:

Lord of all glory and majesty, I come to You this day in the Name of Jesus, *knowing that because of Him I have Your immediate attention. Glory to You and Your wondrous wisdom in all things.*

Father, I am conscious of the gaps in my understanding of Your deeper truths, but I am also aware that the Holy Spirit within me has no such lack. I ask for an in-depth teaching on Christ in me and all that truth suggests. Also, Father, I want to know more about Your laws, especially about the law of the Spirit of life and the law of sin and death. I can see, Father, how I can use these laws under Your auspices to help the helpless, find the lost, heal the sick, cleanse the leper, raise the dead and cast out demons--everything, Father, that will help set the captives free.

Show me also, Father, how I can be an instrument of Your peace, how I can so cooperate with the Christ in me that I will be a walking portrait of His perfect love, joy, peace, gentleness and goodness. Yes, Father, all this I ask in the Name of Jesus--*the Name above every name.*   *Amen--and Amen*

Whatsoever ye shall ask the Father
Read John 16:23,24

"Whatsoever ye shall ask the Father in My Name, He will give it [to] you. Hitherto have ye asked nothing in My Name: ask, and ye shall receive, that your joy may be full." Whatever you are asking God to do for you, are you asking Him in the Name of Jesus?

Tragically, I have heard many people say, "I go directly to God, myself" or "I don't use any middleman: I go right to the Source," which can only be attributed to vanity or ignorance or both. Take heed, beloved, if your prayers don't seem to be going anywhere, or are going unanswered, or seem to be bouncing off the ceiling. If you are not going to the Father through Jesus Christ you can see where your problem might lie.

Just after the Passover meal in the upper room, Jesus tells His disciples He will be leaving them and they will not be able to follow Him. He then gives them a new commandment, that they love one another, telling them that is how men will know that they are His disciples. After this, there is the discourse with Peter and the prophecy that Peter will deny Him three times.

Jesus then tells them not to be troubled, that as they believe in God, they should *believe also in Him*, that in His Father's house are many mansions; that He was going to prepare a place for them (and us); and further, that He would come again and receive them and us to Himself, that all of us could be together with Him and the Father in heaven.

Jesus also said, "And whither I go ye know, and the way ye know" (John 14:4). And here we see why Thomas was given the name Doubting Thomas. Jesus had just finished telling the disciples, including Thomas, that He was going away to His Father's house, where there are many mansions, to prepare a place for them (in heaven), where they can be with Him forever. And Thomas says, "We know not whither Thou goest; and how can we know the way?"

Now here comes the good stuff. Not only did Jesus answer Thomas personally, I believe He did it with great loving patience. For He said, "I am *the* way, *the* truth, and *the* life: *No man cometh to the Father, but by Me*. If ye had known Me, ye should have known My Father also: and from henceforth ye know Him, and have seen Him" (John 13:33-38; 14:1-7).

If indeed Jesus is, as He said, the way, the truth, the life and the only way to get to the Father, why would anyone want to take the

chance that He is somehow wrong or has overstated His importance? He is not wrong, of course; nor has He overstated His position. All of the truth of who Jesus is, the manifested presence of God
in human form, is told in glorious brevity: "If ye had known Me, ye
should have known the Father also: and *from henceforth ye know
Him, and have seen Him*" (John 14:7). In other words, when you are
looking at Jesus, you are looking right at the Father.

   For those who tend to think as I think and to question as I question, "Why would you have to go through God the Son to get to God
the Father?" I have the greatest four-word answer in the world: *Because He said so*. Why fight the issue? Learn the total significance of
using the *Name of Jesus*. It will make you whole; it will restore your
prosperity; it will establish your perfect peace.

He that believeth on Me
Read John 14:12-14

There is that wonderful passage, so simple as to be astonishing,
which gives us the foundation for God's big truth. Jesus is speaking:
"Verily, verily, I say unto you [*you*, beloved], He that believeth on
Me, the works that I do shall he do also; and greater works than
these shall he do; because I go unto My Father. And whatsoever ye
shall ask in My name, that will I do, that the Father may be glorified
in the Son. If ye shall ask anything in My name, I will do it." Then
Jesus says, "And in that day ye shall ask Me nothing. Verily, verily, I
say unto you, Whatsoever ye shall ask the Father in My name, He
will give it you" (John 16:23). In order for you to grasp where I am
headed here, I highly recommend that you reread John 14:6-18 and
John 16:22-28.

   Understand, beloved, others may wish to interpret these passages in a different way. Feel free. I am writing what this is saying to
me, and it thrills my heart.

   Jesus has just told His disciples that He is *the way, the truth and
the life* (John 14:6)--not *a* way, one of *many* truths, a *little bit* of life--
but the only way, the only truth and the only life, without whom we

would immediately die and turn back to dust. He then sets Himself positionally for all time, telling us that no one--no matter how smart, how rich, how famous, how exalted--can get to God without going through Him. At which point He drops the world-shaker: He told His disciples (and us), "If ye had known Me, ye should have known My Father also: and from henceforth *ye know Him, and have seen Him*." I don't know about you, but to me He is clearly saying that He is God in the flesh. But apparently that didn't register with Philip, who was standing there listening with both ears. Because Philip says, "Lord [and how could he call Him Lord and not understand?], show us the Father, and we will believe You. We will consider that sufficient." Generous of him, wouldn't you say? But isn't that much like we are, saying, "If I can see it, touch it, taste it or smell it--maybe even if I can hear it--I will also believe"?

Jesus then asked Philip this question: "After I have been with you all this time, you still don't know Me? Anyone who has seen Me has seen God. So how can you ask to see the Father? Don't you understand that I am in the Father and the Father in Me? And the words I speak are His words? If you don't understand this, why don't you believe Me because of the works I do. It is important that you know this, because the works I do will you do also--and even greater works than these--because I will be in heaven monitoring, approving and sanctifying these deeds.

"While I am here, you can ask anything in My Name, and I will do it to show the glory of God. If you ask Me anything, using My power of attorney, which is My Name, I will do it--provided, of course, you know and keep My commandments because of your love for Me."

Then, in that same sequence, He tells them/us that He will pray that the Father will give still another Comforter, even the Holy Spirit, who will abide with them/us forever. "That Holy Spirit now abides with you in human form," He says, "which is I Myself, and He will be in you in spiritual form when I go to sit at the right hand of the Majesty on high. From there, I will send Him to you. I will not leave you comfortless; that is the way I will come to you--by the Spirit of God."

Then He is saying, in effect, "Because I have told you all these things, you are in grief and heaviness. Nevertheless, I will see you again and you will rejoice. That is the true joy that no one can take from you: it is My personal joy, couched in the Holy Spirit. Then in that day--that day when I am with the Father in heaven and you will not be able to speak to Me face to face--you will not be able to ask anything of Me, personally. At that time, you will be speaking directly to My Father, using My Name as your power of attorney, and He will give you whatsoever you ask. In the past you have not used My Name. It wasn't available as a tool or key. But at the time I am referring to now--what I refer to as *that day*--you will ask and you will receive, that you may greatly rejoice in the fullness of His abundant supply.

"Heretofore I spoke to you often in parables and proverbs, but at the time I am talking about, that will no longer be necessary. Because when I come again, I will clearly reveal the Father; and there will be no need that I pray for you. Because you have loved Me and know that I came from the God of heaven directly to you, God Himself will flood you with His love.

"Now I conclude this by reaffirming: I came forth from God into the world; and now I am leaving the world to go back to Him. My work is completely complete: it is perfectly perfect" (John 16:22-28 author's paraphrase).

When Jesus, the divine Son, instructs us to use His Name in our communications with the Father, we can pretty well know He is not setting forth some whimsical doctrine or fanciful whoop-de-doo. This is real. But the question arises: "Do you know when and how we are to use His Name? And do we know what to expect and under what circumstances?" Whether or not you know and/or understand, let me here share the good stuff with you anyhow. Read on . . .

The kingdom of God is within you
Read Luke 17:20,21

When the Pharisees demanded to know when the kingdom of God would come, Jesus answered them: "The kingdom of God cometh not with observation: neither shall they say, Lo here. or, Lo there. for, behold, the kingdom of God is within you."

That is quite a statement, isn't it? Throughout the gospels of Matthew, Mark and Luke, Jesus makes numerous references to the *kingdom of God* and the *kingdom of heaven*, which most scholars tell us are interchangeable. For whatever reason, although there are some eighty mentions of them in the three gospels, in John these terms appear only twice, and both references are in chapter three, where Jesus is talking to Nicodemus.

This sets up what we might consider a mystery. On the one hand, Jesus tells us the kingdom of God is at hand--that it belongs to the poor and those persecuted for righteousness' sake; that there are those who are least and those who are the greatest in the kingdom of heaven; that it can suffer violence; that we are to seek it first; that it is given to us to know the mysteries of it; that it is like a mustard seed; that it is for little children; that it is difficult for the rich to enter therein. . . . All this, and I haven't gotten through half of Matthew.

When one considers all of this--and that Jesus told the Pharisees the kingdom of God was/is in them, and that there is a great reward to those who leave home and family for the sake of the kingdom--it is difficult to imagine *ooshing* all this into the frail, quavering Christian on the outer fringes of the charismatic walk. But Jesus clearly tells us that it is given to us to know the mysteries of the kingdom of God (Luke 8:10).

So, beloved, it is our move. The ball is in our court, so to speak. And where would you like to go from here? What if I say to you, "Let's get back to basics; let's get back to the Name of Jesus"? How do basics and the Name of Jesus relate to the kingdom of God?

Jesus, speaking to Nicodemus, said that only those who are born-again are able to *see* the kingdom of God (John 3:3) and only those who are born of water and the Spirit can *enter into* the kingdom of God (John 3;5,6). Then, as we wander slowly through the verses that follow, the Word shows us a remarkable series of truths. Among them are:

1) He that is born of the flesh is flesh, and he that is born of the (Holy) Spirit is spirit;

2) We should not be astonished by the fact that Jesus said, "Ye must be born again," for if He had not regarded it as essential to our best interest, He would not have made so much of it;

3) When Nicodemus was incredulous at this seemingly new doctrine, Jesus told him that if he had heard and seen miraculous things and couldn't receive them, how then would it be possible for him to receive heavenly things;

4) Jesus said to Nicodemus, "And no man hath ascended up to heaven, but he that came down from heaven, even the Son of man which *is in heaven*" (John 3:13)--and there He is, standing right there on earth talking to Nicodemus! How does that grab you?'

5) Just as Moses cast the bronze serpent and placed it on a pole and raised it aloft so the people could see it and be healed, so He (Jesus) must be lifted up (on the cross) so the world could be healed;

6) Jesus tells us *why* He came: so that everyone who believed in Him wouldn't have to perish, but could have eternal or everlasting life;

7) Jesus tells us *how* He came: through the love of God for the world, and then, "For God so loved the world, that He *gave* [and here again He is using the past tense concerning Himself while He was standing and speaking in the there

and then] His only begotten Son, that whosoever believeth
in Him should not perish, but have everlasting life";

8) Jesus tells us He didn't come to condemn the world but that
the world through Him might be saved--or experience salvation for their souls--or be redeemed (bought back by
His sacrifice) from everlasting torment;

10) Jesus gives us another glorious revelation when He says to
Nicodemus), "He that believeth on Him [Jesus, the Son] is
not condemned: but he that believeth not is condemned
already, because he hath not believed in the Name of the
only begotten Son of God";

11) Jesus tells us that when He came as the light, men loved
darkness because their deeds were evil and they didn't
want them known;

12) "He that doeth the truth cometh to the light, that his deeds
may be made manifest [that they can be seen by all and
that everyone would know], that they are wrought in [or
by] God."

In our own experience, we have seen hundreds healed as we invoked
the Name of Jesus--laying on hands in the Name of Jesus, rebuking
and commanding in the Name of Jesus, delivering and setting free in
the Name of Jesus, using our faith in His grace, goodness, mercy and
love in the Name of Jesus, agreeing, believing and receiving in the
Name of Jesus.

When the Lord first introduced me to His healing ministry, one
of the first things He showed me was the far-reaching power and
authority of His Name and the superlative interaction of the blessed
Holy Spirit, which is God's love in the midst of us.

My wife and I became even more sharply aware of this at Dr.
Kenneth Hagin's 1975 Camp Meeting in Tulsa. At the end of one of
the services, hundreds of people lined up all the way around the
auditorium for healing. And as Hagin was going down the line, laying hands on the afflicted (invoking the Name of Jesus), people

began to fall in the Spirit before he even touched them. Then he
began to move faster and the people began to fall faster--until he
was almost running.

There wasn't time enough for the whole phrase, "in the Name
of Jesus," so Brother Hagin, often barely touching the people,
shouted, "The Name . . . the Name . . . the Name!" People were falling like dominoes. If what was happening hadn't been so important,
it would have been amusing. In fact, I admit it: it was amusing--
Kenneth zipping along in the Spirit; Oretha, his wife, trying to keep
pace, laying cloths over the legs of the women; the ushers stumbling
and falling over each other trying to catch the people before they hit
the ground. It was something to watch--sort of Spirit inspired mayhem. Oh, but how many were gloriously healed and set free from
bondages.

I will give unto thee the keys of the kingdom
Read Matthew 16:19

"I will give unto thee the keys of the kingdom of heaven." If the
kingdom of God is within me, why do I need keys to get in? Mostly,
beloved, because we don't have the foggiest notion what that means
(in the natural)--nor what are the potential consequences. In my
opinion, we have already been given the keys: they are already ours--
but we haven't located the locks they fit. We know, of course, they
have nothing to do with any normal locking mechanism--that they
are actually the keys to binding and loosing everything that can be
classified as "whatsoever." What, pray tell, is a whatsoever?

It is vital that we grasp what Jesus is saying here: "I will give
unto thee the keys of the kingdom of heaven: and *whatsoever* thou
shalt bind on earth shall be bound in heaven: and *whatsoever* thou
shalt loose on earth shall be loosed in heaven." Notice, beloved, that
He says *whatsoever*--and not *whomsoever*. Although both are pro-
nouns, there is an important distinction: a *whatsoever* can be a
human, animal, thing, place or activity--while *whomsoever* normally
relates to people.

The reason I am belaboring the point is this: Jesus gave us the keys of the kingdom so that we would be able to bind and loose *whatsoevers*: demons, sickness, suffering, pain, allergies, strife, confusion, discord, unpleasantness of any kind, business, industry, employee relations, finances, poverty or abundance. . . . If you can name it, you can bind and/or loose it. How and why? By your words--because you have been given *the keys*. They are your symbol of authority. Just as in ancient times when a conqueror took a city without destroying it, his symbol of authority or conquest was the keys to the gates of that city--given over to him by the vanquished king or potentate.

How does that apply to you and me? In the Word, Paul asks us a question and gives us his answer: "Who [or *whatsoever*--in my version] shall separate us from the love of Christ? Shall tribulation, or distress, or persecution, or famine, or nakedness, or peril, or sword? As it is written, For Thy sake we are killed all the day long; we are accounted as sheep for the slaughter. Nay, in all these things [whatsoevers] we are more than conquerors through Him [God] that loved us. For I am persuaded, that neither death, nor life, nor angels, nor principalities, nor powers, nor things present, nor things to come, nor height, nor depth, nor any other creature [all *whatsoevers*], shall be able to separate us from the love of God, which is in Christ Jesus our Lord" (Romans 8:35-39).

The Word affirms that we are more than conquerors through Him (God) who loved us. And how do we get to God? Through Jesus Christ who is the way, the truth and the life. What gets us there? Our symbols of authority, the keys. And how did we get the keys? Jesus gave them to us along with His power of attorney, His Name--the Name that is above every name. Isn't that stunning?

In the following examples of how to use the Name of Jesus, you might wish to insert your own names, titles, descriptions and identifications. Remember, these are illustrations only. And I will be speaking to things, circumstances, afflictions, businesses, finances--even the weather--as examples:

You listen to me, you (whatsoever thing, object, condition), for I am speaking to you in the Name of Jesus and I am commanding you to line up with the Word of God. And I say to you that henceforth you will have no influence in my life-- neither spiritually, physically, mentally nor emotionally. Because of my complete authority to use the Name of Jesus I not only declare it to be so--but I count it done.

<u>In the matter of circumstances (whether need or desire, illness or injury)</u>: *In the Name of Jesus, I say to my (your, his, her, their) spirit man, "Be healthy and whole according to God's Word and reject any further attempts by the evil one to afflict you and that which you have received. " I say to those heal-thy cells of my body, "You attack those symptoms and dissolve that [whatever, if you can name it] and take away all soreness. And because the Name of Jesus is above you, you must obey and be gone."*

<u>For the one in critical condition</u>: *In the Name of Jesus, I speak to your spirit man and I command you to live and not die. "For the law of the Spirit of life in Christ Jesus hath made you free from the law of sin and death."*

<u>In business matters (whether buying, selling or making a prof-it)</u>: *In the Name of Jesus, I am calling you into my possession. Because of God's love and His promise to supply all of my needs according to His riches in glory--and you are a specific need--I am calling you mine. And lest you doubt, I am using God's instruction to me and following His example by calling those things that be not as though they were. So I say again, "You are mine" or "I thank my God in the Name of Jesus that I can call you sold. You are an excellent buy--therefore someone will highly desire to own you. They will consider you a perfect possession and you will grace*

their house (basement, garage, driveway, whatever). They will consider your color (style, shape, form, whatever) perfect for their need or circumstance--and you will be a delight to them."

<u>Regarding financial matters:</u> *I thank You, Father, that because of the Name of Jesus You can take my words and give them substance. I can speak to those financial mountains in my life and command that they be cast into the sea, according to Mark 11:23. Because I have the wisdom of God, I can freely say to you, you mountain of debt (confusion, bondage, whatever), "Be dissolved in Jesus' Name."* Now begin the creative process of forming a new image of success.

<u>For those who have a problem praying for weather changes-- always wondering about the possible adverse effect a change will have on someone else--I can only tell you this: God knoweth. So here goes:</u> *Heavenly Father, possessor of heaven and earth, I come before You as a child, invoking the Name of Jesus in the matter of the weather. With Your permission, Father, I am going to speak to the rain clouds and command them to form in this area. And I thank You, Father, that because of Your Word and the Name of Jesus-- and the fact that I will not doubt in my heart but will believe that those things which I say will come to pass--those clouds will not only come but will bring an abundance of rain for those in need--while in areas where rain would be harmful, it will be scant. Now you rain clouds, I speak to you in the Name of Jesus and I command you to begin to form over this area [whatever area you designate]. And I say to you, Bring an abundance of rain--all that is needed or desired. Hold not back--neither form in the places stipulated not to have rain. You must obey because I have invoked the Name of Jesus--and, therefore, I consider it done.*

I don't have any way of knowing how all this is going to set with you but I certainly hope you will get a witness in your spirit that this is one way to become a successful overcomer. Some of you, of course, will think it is far out to speak to inanimate objects and circumstances. But it isn't all that strange when you consider the things Jesus spoke to: the storm, the fig tree, the dead (the widow's son and Lazarus) and the legion of demons in the demoniac at Gadara.

When He spoke, things happened: the storm ceased its fury, the fig tree dried up from the root, the widow's son and Lazarus arose from the dead and the demons departed into the two thousand swine, which rushed into the sea and drowned. God expects us to speak to things and circumstances in the same way Jesus did, and to enjoy the identical success. Not one tiny whit less. As I have pointed out before, all the power and authority that opened the Red Sea and raised Jesus from the dead is resident in us.

In closing this chapter, beloved, there is one imperative I will set before you: at no time and under no conditions are we to use this power/authority medium as a means of testing God. For one thing, the Bible tells us quite clearly that God cannot be tested (James 1:13), which implies that He cannot be tempted, tested or tried. Nor does He use any form of whatsoever to tempt, test or try us: that just isn't His way. He is forever loving and drawing us to Himself and toward a higher level of achievement so that through His Word and the Name of Jesus we can be the light of the world.

That is how we become more than conquerors--by being the beloved children of the King of kings and the Lord of lords. For no matter how great the conquest, the conqueror is always subject to the Highest Authority. And, as you know, we are to rule and reign with Him. Phenomenal!

12
Healing, Health and Wholeness
By the Sovereign Work of the Holy Spirit Alone

The Spirit of the Lord is upon Me
Read Luke 4:18-21

"The Spirit of the Lord is upon Me [Jesus proclaimed in the synagogue at Nazareth as He read from the book of the prophet Isaiah] because He hath anointed Me to preach the gospel to the poor; He hath sent Me to heal the brokenhearted, to preach deliverance to the captives, and recovering of sight to the blind, to set at liberty them that are bruised, to preach the acceptable year of the Lord. And He closed the book, and He gave it again to the minister, and sat down. And the eyes of all them that were in the synagogue were fastened on Him. And He began to say unto them, This day is this scripture fulfilled in your ears."

In this final chapter, we will be dealing with healing, health and wholeness through the sovereign working of the Holy Spirit (or Holy Ghost) acting alone (without any seeming contribution from man).

Those who have had the privilege of being in a service where the Holy Spirit has moved with His dynamite (*dunamis*) power will testify to the awe-inspiring wonder of His love. Cancer, multiple sclerosis, diabetes, ulcers, blindness, deafness, vertebrate diseases, internal and external afflictions--you name it--just dissolve, disintegrate or disappear in the twinkling of an eye. And, oh, what it does to the heart of the observer! It is unforgettable.

Probably the most notable catalyst of this phenomenon in our time was the late Kathryn Kuhlman. What an experience to be in one of her healing services! Nevertheless, by her own admission, she was forever mystified (though thrilled) at the awesome intervention of the Holy Spirit in her meetings.

After several years of searching, in the final weeks before I gave my heart to the Lord, I went to one of Kathryn's meetings at the First Episcopal Church in Pittsburgh. And I have never been the same since.

Being an unbeliever at the time--albeit an enthusiastic seeker/ explorer, having seen a friend's life completely changed by a Kathryn Kuhlman service--I just had to go and see for myself what it was all about.

I came away from there stunned to the socks. I had only seen Miss Kuhlman one time on television and, quite honestly, she turned me off. I now know, of course, that it was that old serpent, called the Devil and Satan (Revelation 12:9), trying to deceive me into believing that all this was bunk and that I had better be very careful or some of that fanaticism would rub off on me. But having been under that cloud of fraudulent trickery so many years--and now with the love of God and His light piercing the gloom--I had begun to suspect that there was something more out there than I was seeing. And was there ever!

The excitement began at 7:30 A.M. on a Friday in October, 1970. I was strolling casually toward the church--wondering what kind of idiot I was, going at 7:30 to an 11:00 service--when I saw a huge crowd up in the next block. I remember wondering what was going on. Was there some great tragedy? Was the church on fire? I didn't see any smoke. But the closer I got the more I was aware that something astonishing must be happening--or was certainly in the making. There must have been three thousand people on the sidewalk in front of the church and the excited anticipation was so overwhelming it sent shivers up my spine.

I later learned that people had come from all over the world to be at this meeting. They had come by plane, by bus, by taxi and on foot. They had come in braces, in wheelchairs, in joyous wonder and curiosity--and not a few in pain and suffering. Like Nicodemus (John 3:9), I wondered, *How can these things be? What is happening here? What am I looking at?*

One of the many wonders of that day was the fact that, due to the great number of people crowding the sidewalk and spilling out into the street, the people in charge were forced to open the doors two hours early. People quite literally *poured* into the church. It was like an organized mob scene. Only instead of everyone rushing to get out, they were rushing to get in and be seated. It was only by the grace of God that the slow and elderly weren't trampled under foot. Do you suppose that mammoth act of controlled grace was orchestrated by the Holy Spirit? Of course. Who else?

Neither before nor since have I ever experienced the like of that day. Five thousand people in a state of excited anticipation that seemed boundless. There was joy unspeakable, great wonder and amazement, astonishment of heart, and spine-tingling awe, and I was experiencing it all.

Promptly at eleven, the organ sounded and a great hush fell on the auditorium, followed by the many-voiced choir singing "He Touched Me." The next sound I became aware of was my own gulping sobs as the Spirit of God began to cut through my surrounding clouds of darkness. I didn't know that was what was happening, of course, but every note on the keyboard of my emotions, from lowest bass to highest treble, was repeatedly struck by the deft fingers of the Almighty God who loved me--me of all people. About mid-song or perhaps the second chorus the whole congregation joined in and I was devastated. I all but collapsed somewhere between joy unspeakable and abject condemnation, at once thrilled to be in such an atmosphere of love and astonished at God's allowing me the privilege. And though I had no such concept at the time, I now know it was God's battle--that He personally fought for me through Jesus Christ--and that He won, which allowed me to win. Glory to God--and hallelujah!

The second song that morning was "How Great Thou Art," in the midst of which Kathryn came onto the platform in a gorgeous, multicolored full-length gown and led the singing to its conclusion-- by which time I was almost wholly drained. Since I was in an aisle seat, if there had been a fire, the people would have had to climb over me. I don't believe I could have moved a muscle.

Kathryn was a smash. At the time, she must have been in her early seventies and was long and lean, lithe and graceful. Even up close she could have passed for fifty. Tootsie and I later came to know her through being on her program. She constantly amazed us with her agility and joyous enthusiasm for life and what the Lord was doing in and through her ministry.

But on this particular morning I was there alone--*or so I thought*--alternately laughing and crying, listening to past testimonies of healing and generally being part of the whole scene. It was wonderful. It was awful. It was glorious. It was soul-wrenching.

Then Kathryn began to preach about Jesus. It was a simple message, as I recall--not world-shaking. After about fifteen to twenty minutes of speaking, she stopped abruptly--right in mid-sentence-- and pointed her long, bony finger toward the balcony and said, "There's a woman up there with thick glasses. Take them off, honey. You'll be able to see better without them." Then, pointing in another direction, she said, "There is a man over here to my right wearing a hearing aid. Take it off, sir; you'll be able to hear better without it." Again pointing, this time right down in front of her, she said, "There's a gentleman down here in the front with a long-time stomach ulcer. You've just been healed."

As she went on and on, calling out healings--with her very sensitive ushers bringing people forward for testimonies--the excitement and anticipation grew. Along with her calling out healings by the word of knowledge, there was the sovereign move of the Spirit of God as it hovered over the entire congregation. People began to shout for joy as they were healed and set free right where they sat. I suppose it could be called orderly pandemonium. All over the auditorium the ushers were interviewing those who were healed, so they could bring them to the front. Then Kathryn would invite some to the microphone to tell how great things the Lord had done for them. It was tremendous and I kept wondering where the news media was. Why weren't things like this reported? The hokey negative stuff they usually report is so without character or appeal--why not a little good news for a change?

The Kathryn Kuhlman meeting went on for four-and-a-half hours--yet the time sped so swiftly as to seem no more than minutes. It was that dynamic. And no one who went there came out of that meeting the same. Lives were changed dramatically. There is no way one can be a part of something like that and remain the same. And that is just a part of the ministry of the Holy Spirit--the third Person of the Trinity--who supplied the power (*dunamis*) of creation; who gave the light God called for; who brought into being every living thing; who is the moving force of God's supply train; who supplied that strong east wind that divided the Red Sea; who inspired the written Word of God; who raised Jesus from the dead and who is resident in you and me. And for you who are fighting sickness, affliction or disease: He is the force that can drive them out of you. It was He who was given to Jesus in unlimited measure, who supplied the anointing that allowed Jesus to go about "doing good, and healing all who were oppressed of the devil."

But ye shall receive power
Read Acts 1:8,9

"But ye shall receive power after that the Holy Ghost is come upon you," Jesus told His disciples just before "He was taken up; and a cloud received Him out of their sight" (Acts 1:8,9). This doesn't mean that He would be siphoning off some of His power (or authority) in order to give it to you and me. While still retaining all the power that was given Him in heaven and earth (Matthew 28:18), He was able to give it all to us. How is that possible? How can He keep it and still have us own it?

As I have written before, *we are Jesus in the earth, we are the body of Christ*, and the authority He has given us works on the same principle as *love*--the more you give the more you get, until one day even *you* will not be able to distinguish the difference between you and Him. There will be no difference, because the work of the Holy Spirit is to help us become conformed to His image. Knowing that would surely come to pass--because God never fails--He was able freely to take His place beside the throne of God as the first-born of many brethren (which includes you and me).

So, beloved, how is it possible for you to have sickness or disease in your body--a body filled to overflowing with the power and love of Almighty God? Are you indeed filled with the power and love of Almighty God? If you are suffering any form of affliction, beloved, know that these questions are not meant to foster fear and doubt but to guide you (by the Holy Ghost) to the truth of God-- which is Jesus, the way, the truth and the life, remember?

In the matter of finding the way, the Holy Spirit will guide you: in coming to know the truth, the Holy Spirit will show you; and in embracing the fundamental elements that make up life, the Holy Spirit will reveal them. His greatest desire is identical to God's: to have intimate and joyous fellowship with you. And as you open your heart to Him, He will open to you the treasures of wisdom and knowledge, insights into the mysteries of the kingdom, penetrating recognition of the deep things of God.

Why does He want all these things for you? And why do they seem so difficult to grasp? From His perspective, of course, He adores us at any stage of our spiritual development, whether we remain children or go on toward maturity. But our closest walk with Him is going to be in the growth pattern where we are constantly seeking more and more to develop not only our *agape* (love) relationship but our *phileo* (love) relationship--that wondrous Father/son relationship that is so precious in His sight.

In the light of what Jesus told His disciples, "Ye shall receive power after that the Holy Ghost has come upon you" (Acts 1:8), if you are a Spirit-filled believer, what are you doing with all the power you have been given? Are you using it to knock off the old boy, the deceiver, the accuser of the brethren, that liar, cheat, thief and murderer, the dragon, that old serpent, called the devil and Satan? Or are you allowing him to dump all his garbage on you?

Remember, beloved, the only authority the devil has over a believer is that which the believer allows. If you allow him to put sickness on you, he will--and if you allow him to kill you, he will. He is absolutely unscrupulous. Whatever dastardly thing you will sanction, that will he do. For just as God's nature is love, Satan's is hatred. One among the manifold reasons the Holy Spirit was given was so that, like Jesus, we could put the devil under our feet. How? By doing exactly as Jesus did--by telling him in no uncertain terms, "It is written: All power is given unto me in heaven and earth--so get lost, you foul thing, in the Name of Jesus."

In order to pursue a closer and more intimate relationship with Almighty God--which can be done only through the Name of Jesus and ongoing fellowship with the Holy Spirit--I would suggest you pray something like this:

Heavenly Father, glorious Lord, I come before You with praise and thanksgiving and not a little awe. I see Your mighty hand and stretched-out arm wielding power beyond man's understanding: guiding the whole earth in its great oval arc through the heavens; moving the clouds where You will; causing it to rain on the just and the unjust; having in Your keeping the mysteries of the universal order that gives balance to the atmosphere surrounding us; and by Your Spirit controlling those things we know not so that we can be comfortable with those things we know; by Your might and dominion directing the majestic so that we can regulate the mundane. What a wonder You are, Father, what a great and glorious wonder You are, having made provision for all men for all time--even to the end of the world. . . .

*Now, Father, I have this desire in my heart: to know and
have an intimate relationship with the Holy Spirit; to hear His
whispered instructions and be instantly obedient to His charge;
to formulate all plans and undertakings in perfect harmony with
His desires for me; to be delicately sensitive to His guiding light
as it leads me through the labyrinthine passageways of my life.*

*And, Father, I want to know the mind of the Spirit as it re-
lates to my personal healing, health and wholeness. I know it is
Your desire that I should enjoy the fullness of life and the relaxed
contentment of Your perfect peace. But in order to do that, Father, I need the positive intervention of Your Holy Spirit--either
acting sovereignly on His own or by teaching me where and how
to participate. For all this bounty, Father, I again thank and
praise and glorify You in the Name that is above every name--the
Name of Jesus Christ of Nazareth.*   *Amen--and Amen*

Go thy way
Read Read Matthew 8:5-13; Mark 7:24-30

"Go thy way." That is what Jesus told both the centurion in Matthew
8:5-13 and the Syrophoenician woman in Mark 7:24-30. Just what are
we being shown in these two examples? In neither case did Jesus
seem to take any action personally. Yet by the time the centurion got
back to his house, the palsy had left his grievously tormented servant. And by the time the woman had reached her house, her daughter had been totally set free from the demon. Since Jesus didn't
come near the afflicted ones, how were they set free? Was it by the
sovereign working of the Holy Spirit? Or was it something the centurion or the woman *did*?

To the centurion, Jesus said, "Go thy way; and as thou hast
believed, so be it done unto thee" (Matthew 8:13). And to the woman, He said, "For this saying go thy way; the devil is gone out of thy
daughter" (Mark 7:29). Can you see any correlation there? I don't.
Yet both situations have this in common: the victims were set free.

In other chapters of this book, reference has been made to God's omnipresence (His being present everywhere in all the universe at all times), which is why what we say and do sometimes has implications of enormous importance across the earth and around the world. You see, beloved, because there is neither time nor distance in the kingdom of God and because the Lord Jesus has assured us we get what we say in line with His Word, we have the authority to send the manifested healing virtue of God anywhere on earth. That does not mean that God and His healing presence is not already there. But our speaking does give Him legal jurisdiction over that situation, whether sickness, disease or affliction. However, this still doesn't allow Him dominion over the personal fears and doubts of that individual. So if it is in your heart to send such a prayer for healing across the earth, remember to bind up fear and doubt and to loose peace, joy and love into the transaction so the Spirit of God can work in perfect universal harmony with the force of faith.

Where the centurion's servant and the Syrophoenician woman's daughter were concerned, the scriptures give no evidence that Jesus addressed either the servant's palsy or the daughter's demon. But it appears that He used the centurion's faith and obedience and the woman's persistence and obedience. For neither of them questioned, "What if? . . . " They simply went their way, expecting His instructions to produce victory.

Time and again we are shown the awesome power of the Holy Spirit when people are obedient. When the Spirit of God spoke up in Abram (later to become Abraham), his obedience gave him the position of father of the faithful throughout all generations; Moses' obedience to "lift thou up thy rod, and stretch out thine hand over the sea, and divide it" brought the opening of the Red Sea; then there was Joshua, speaking by the Holy Spirit, commanding the sun and moon to stand still, which they did for nearly a whole day; Elijah pronounced judgment on Ahab and Jezebel, withholding the rain for three-and-a-half years, then prayed fervently for the rain to come at last, and when it came, he girded up his loins and ran twenty miles (in the Spirit) and beat Ahab to Jezreel, though Ahab was riding in a chariot; Elisha, by the Spirit, commanded Naaman the leper to wash seven times in Jordan. Naaman, furious because he had traveled a great distance thinking the prophet was going to lay hands on him, finally entered into God's obedience and dipped in Jordan seven times and "his flesh came again like unto the flesh of a little child."

There are so many places in the Bible where the Spirit of God does great and mighty things--defeating the hosts that came against Israel, in some cases causing such confusion in the ranks that their enemies literally killed one another. In the case of Sennacherib and the whole Assyrian army (185,000 men), they were totally destroyed and Sennacherib returned home to be slain by his own sons. That is all pretty big stuff.

How do we regard the Holy Spirit, beloved? Is He some sort of vague entity the writers put in the Bible to fill up space? Does He have a place in your day-to-day life? And do you know what that place is?

In the final analysis, what the Holy Spirit does is what God ordained from the beginning: through Jesus Christ He supplies the all knowledge we are given as a gift from God--the instinctive as well as the cumulative wisdom, knowledge and understanding that is centered in God, including the knowledge of good and evil (handed down to us from the garden of Eden); gives us the consciousness to divide truth from error and a conscience to know which to follow; provides the life forces that sustain and preserve us, forces that science through the centuries has been able to do little more than recognize. And even though scientists know and are able to reproduce every element, they always fail to produce life because of the one essential ingredient--*God the Holy Spirit, the Spirit of life in Christ Jesus*--without which there can be no life. Can you see that, beloved?

When Jesus told both the centurion and the woman, "Go thy way," was He saying, "Go about your business as though nothing was ever wrong in the first place?" Is He saying, "For those who trust in

Me there is nothing too difficult for Me to accomplish in and through that trust?" Is He saying, "Trust in the Lord with all thine heart; and lean not unto thine own understanding?" (Proverbs 3:5). I think He was saying all those things. What is your conclusion?

Of all the books of the Bible, the Psalms of David have the most to say about trusting the Lord. There are more than thirty scriptures that speak of the wisdom of trusting the Lord in all things, exhorting all men to recognize His faithfulness, His mercy and His lovingkindness. And when David was anointed by Samuel at Bethlehem, "The Spirit of the Lord came upon David from that day forward" (1 Samuel 16:13). To say the Psalms are inspired is the understatement of all time. However, we tend to give the credit to David rather than to the Spirit of God. But we humans are prone to lift up man instead of the source of his achievements, the Holy One of Israel, the Spirit of the living God who indwells us.

But His question to us is how far will we trust Him? How long will we endure any form of affliction before we run to the medicine cabinet, the doctor or the hospital? Do we seek the Lord before we do any of these things? Do we say, "Lord, I thank You that You have shown that no sickness or affliction is from above but is quite likely a vain imagination from the evil one"?

Your response to these questions is all-important to your rate of recovery, to your ability to overcome whatever afflictions are trying to attach themselves to your body. If you are having problems with this, you want to have a direct and personal relationship with the Comforter (John 14:16-26; 15:26; 16:7). The Greek word used here is *parakletos*, meaning "one called alongside [to help and therefore comfort--to give peace or set at ease]."

If you are a born-again, Spirit-filled believer and there is an uneasiness in your inner man (spirit man), then you should ask yourself, "Am I fearful or afraid? Am I doubting the enablement God has given me to overcome? Am I giving place to the devil through concentrating too much on myself and the affliction I feel?" If your answer to any of these questions is yes, then you need to have a

serious talk with the Holy Spirit, reminding Him that He is to guide
you into all truth. God promised you that and He will keep His word
in all things, including your need to know. After all, that is as much a
need as any other, even a greater need in some instances. So tell
Him, beloved, not in an arrogant way but certainly with authority.
For what God promises, He will most assuredly give--or else there
would be no need for Him to watch over His Word to perform it.

God is a Spirit
Read John 4:24

"God is a Spirit, and they that worship Him must worship Him in
spirit and in truth." Jesus was speaking to the Samaritan woman at
Jacob's well in the city of Sychar. This entire incident follows closely
on the heels of His first miracle at Cana, turning the water to wine;
His first passover at Jerusalem after the beginning of His ministry;
His first driving of the money-changers and sacrificial animal bro-
kers out of the temple; His first admission (to Nicodemus) to being
the Son of God, followed by the testimony of John the Baptist that
He (Jesus) had been given the Spirit of God without measure; His
first recorded statement (to the woman at the well in Sychar) that
He was/is the Messiah (the Anointed One).

The reason this statement about God being a Spirit is so important to us is centered in what we are. We were created in the express
image of God (Genesis 1:26; Hebrews 1:3) and, like Him, we are
spirits also. However, God is a Spirit (capitalized), while we are
spirits who have souls and live in mortal bodies as the body of Christ
who is the express image of the living God. Any of you want to take
a shot at how that works?

From my perspective, I see this as one of the great mysteries
that we will be shown when we stand before the throne in our glorified bodies. Only then will it be possible for us to know the fullness
of what we truly are right this moment. Clearly we are already what
the Bible says we are. But what we have yet to learn is how we will
be affected by the progressive revelations that are unfolding so fast

and furiously. For there have been more revelations of God's truths in the past ten years than there had been in the last six thousand years (from 4004 B.C., as some scholars figure it).

Regardless of such extraordinary tidbits of information--publishers, scholars, teachers and Bible study groups, notwithstanding--the born-again, Spirit-filled believer is already what God has forecast him/her to be from that beginning--and nothing by any means can change that. Why? Because God has always known the end from the beginning: nothing is just not a progressive happenstance. We are struggling to understand what we are and are to become. However, our flights of fancy are forever being launched from the wrong plateau (Webster defines *plateau* as a "flat thing")--our heads. As long as we and our activities are controlled by our heads (rather than our hearts, spirits or inner man), we will forever be at the mercy of our intellect, which is infinitesimal indeed. But through our hearts, spirits or inner man, the Holy Spirit is able to pour all of His wisdom, knowledge, understanding and power for His purposes in our service to the living God.

Now for the wind down, beloved. As you will have clearly recognized, this book has one thing in common with the Bible: it was written *to you*, God's beloved children. Beyond that, its purposes can be said to parallel God's purposes in acquainting you with His love, goodness, mercy and His heart's desire to see to your personal healing, health and wholeness. All other benefits you have gained in the process of reading and application--in praying for others as well as yourselves--should be counted as pluses.

For you who have not fully grasped the significance of joining yourselves to a partnership with the blessed Holy Spirit--thereby helping plan the highway for our God and the second coming of His Son, the soon coming *King of kings and Lord of lords*--there are a few final things for you to consider.

Most of us know that Jesus is "the true Light, which lighteth every man that cometh into the world" (John 1:9). But too often we are like pilot lights hidden behind the bottom panel of the hot-water heater or under the center strip of the stove. All of us instinctively know we have great potential. But, for the most part, we don't know how to turn up the gas or how to be a burning and a shining light, as Jesus described John the Baptist. Yet it is he who should be our pattern if the Lord has not already given us some other specific ministry.

As born-again, Spirit-filled believers, our roles are almost identical to his--as can be seen in the song of Zachariah, John's father. The song begins with the prophetic role all of us have: "And thou, child, shalt be called the prophet of the Highest: for thou shalt go before the face of the Lord to prepare His ways; to give knowledge of salvation unto His people [the world over] by the remission of their sins, through the tender mercy of our God; whereby the Dayspring from on high hath visited us, to give light to them that sit in darkness and in the shadow of death, to guide our feet into the way of peace" (Luke 1:76-79).

And now, let us have this final prayer together:

Heavenly Father, Glorious Lord, Your Word says You will have mercy on all those who fear (or reverence) You from generation to generation. And, Father, by faith I stand in that place of rest, knowing there is no way You can fail or fall short in any blessing. You are unalterably perfect and Your truth is everlasting to those who love You--including me. Now, Father, I give You all blessings, honor and glory--and in the Name of Jesus, I say,

Amen--and Amen

Afterword

With all that has gone before--the information, the stories, the scriptures and the prayers--we still haven't exhausted the most infinitesimal measure of God's miraculous power of steadfast (unwavering) love. It is so far beyond our comprehension, beloved, that we tend to shun it, mostly because we can't figure it out. What is that need we humans have of trying to understand the inner workings of everything we cannot possibly know--while we refuse to try to fix our own watch bands or rotate our tires?

Our greatest need, of course, is to come to grips with who and what we are in Christ, God's most adored and precious children. For when we come to know the full significance of that and our kingdom privileges, we will be able to freely enter into (and heartily rejoice in) the glory He has set aside for each of us from the foundation of the world.

Could that possibly exclude healing, health and wholeness? Of course not. Neither can we approach these things as being somehow allied to a state of mind or having something to do with mind over matter. It is nothing of the kind. If it is cold and we wish to get warm, we get closer to the fire. The same principle applies when we are sick and want to be well: we get closer to the Healer.

The writer does not suggest that *Wilt Thou Be Made Whole?* is the be all and end all of healing, health and wholeness. In fact, it barely scratches the surface of one of the most exciting aspects of God's love. It is meant to arouse and inspire your curiosity and imaginative enterprise so it will be the launching pad that will get you into God's orbit of joy and gladness.

Following this **Afterword** are what I call **Good confessions**. They are one of many ways you can agree with God and what He says about you. After all, if you are to be His dwelling place, you have to understand His communication system, which makes AT&T seem like a horseless Pony Express. For God communicates instantaneously worldwide, without operators, wires, air waves or satellites, without intricate systems, technical obsolescence or engineering marvels, without hundreds of thousands of employees and monthly billings. It is all free. The only requirement is that you put up your spiritual antenna and tune in to God's program, which is centered in His Word.

Good Confessions

For Healing:

Father, Your Word says, "I am the Lord that healeth thee" (Exodus 15:26). And I know that means me--thank you, Lord.

Soul, I command you, in the Name of Jesus, to, "Bless the Lord, O my soul, and forget not all His benefits, who forgiveth all my iniquities, who healeth all my diseases" (see Psalm 103:2,3).

Glory to You, Father God, for "You sent Your Word, and healed me, and delivered me from my destructions" (see Psalm 107:20).

Bless You, Lord, for inspiring Peter to write, "Who His own self bare my sins in His own body on the tree, that I, being dead to sins, should live unto righteousness: by whose stripes I was healed" (see 1 Peter 2:24).

And oh, how thrilling, Lord: "But unto me that fears Your Name, the Sun of righteousness shall arise with healing in His wings" (see Malachi 4:2).

I thank You, Jesus, that You "went about all Galilee, teaching . . . and preaching . . . and healing all manner of sickness and all manner of disease among the people" as my example of Your lovingkindness to the children of men and to me (Matthew 4:23).

What a Savior! What a Lord! I thank You, Father, that Jesus fulfilled that scripture which says, "Himself took my infirmities and bore my sicknesses" (see Isaiah 53:4) so that I wouldn't have to carry them. That is just thrilling to know (see also Matthew 8:17).

What an eye-opener, my God: "How You anointed Jesus of Nazareth with the Holy Ghost and with power: who went about
   doing good, and healing all that were oppressed of the devil;
   because You were with Him," thereby revealing to me the truth
   of where sicknesses and afflictions come from--and so I will
   know whom and how to fight (see Acts 10:38).
And, Father, I know all this is true, because Your Word tells me,
   "Jesus Christ the same yesterday, and today, and forever"
   (Hebrews 13:8).

For Health:

Blessings and honor and glory to Your Name, my God--because
   Your Word has shown me that I can "Hope in God; for I shall
   yet praise him, who is the health of my countenance, and my
   God" (see Psalm 42:11).
Also, Father, the scriptures assure me that Your Word shall be
   health to my navel--the central core of my being--and health to
   the marrow in my bones, where is the source of the purest
   blood and, thus, my vigor and strength" (see Proverbs 3:8).
And O Father, how concisely Your Words fit my needs, especially
   where You say, "My son, attend to My words; incline thine ear
   unto My sayings. Let them not depart from thine eyes; keep
   them in the midst of thine heart. For they are life unto those
   that find them, and health to all their flesh" (Proverbs 4:20-22).
   Father, help me by Your Spirit to fully understand how I am to
   wholly cooperate with Your Word in these verses.
Heavenly Father, Your infinite sweetness is often portrayed by
   references to honey and so often by the inspiration of Your
   Spirit working through Solomon: "Pleasant words are like an
   honeycomb, sweet to the soul, and health to my bones" (Proverbs 16:24). I covet Your sweetness, my God, that my soul
   shall know Your refreshing and my bones Your health.

Glorious One, my Lord and my God, I ask You to lead into a fast
that You have chosen, "to loose the bands of wickedness, to
undo the heavy burdens, and to let the oppressed go free . . . to
deal thy bread to the hungry, and that thou bring the poor that
are cast out to thy house. . . . Then shall my light break forth as
the morning, and my health shall spring forth speedily: and my
righteousness shall go before me; and the glory of the Lord
shall be my rereward, or my rear guard" (see Isaiah 58:6-8).

And wonder of wonders, my Father, how thrilling when Your Word
calls me "beloved"--as John writes, "Beloved, I wish above all
things that thou shouldest prosper and be in health, even as my
soul prospereth" (3 John 2). I know in my heart those words
were written to me, personally--inspired by Your Holy Spirit.
Glory, Father!

And this from the Psalms, Father, where it says, "Because You have
set Your love upon me . . . with long life will You satisfy me,
and show me Your salvation" (see Psalm 91:14-16), which the
Name of Jesus means, as well as healing, health and wholeness.

And then there is this blessed scripture, God of all glory and majesty: "For in You I live, and move, and have my being" (see Acts
17:28). Lord, I thank You that Your Word says You are my
health, and since You and Your Word are One and You are
divine, I can count it so that I have divine health.

For Wholeness:

In this dimension, Father, I wish to be as Caleb the son of Jephun-
neh: he was given the desires of his heart, because he wholly followed the Lord (Deuteronomy 1:36). Not only did he get the
desires of his heart, he enjoyed robust health when he was
eighty-five years old. Father, I thank You that I can stand on
the truth of Your scriptures, where Jesus says, "They that be
whole need not a physician. . . ." And I say I am whole
(Matthew 9:12).

And Lord, I fearlessly stand on Your word to the woman with the is-
    sue of blood. I can confess that I can "be of good comfort; my
    faith hath made me whole" (see Matthew 9:22).
Glory, glory and hallelujah, my God. When I worship and praise
    You, I can *stand forth*, as Jesus commanded the man with the
    withered hand and have not only my hand made whole but my
    entire being (Mark 3:3-5).
And, Lord God, where the Lord Jesus asked the impotent man,
    "Wilt thou be made whole?" (John 5:6-8). I answer that for
    myself and I say, "Yes, yes, yes!"

Beloved, there are many more scriptures in each of these categories,
but in order for this book to come to a screeching halt, somebody
has to say "when"--which that still small voice just said to me. Selah.